I know at Cambridge
nadian lifting record, the couple
ndred fans there who
rting us athletes
"They gave
lift
رفرفت اعلام ٤٥ دولة فى دوره
الألعاب العالمية للمعوقين • و
افتتح الدورة كـــل من وز
وقد توسط عام السوداز
D1190340
Wheel-chair race at the first annual B.S.A.D. annual Sports Festival
for Physically Handicapped Children held at Stoke Mandeville
SPIRIT OF STOKE MANDEVILLE
THE AIM OF THE 'STOKE MANDEVILLE GAMES IS TO UNITE PARALYSED MEN AND WOMEN FROM ALL PARTS OF THE WORLD IN AN INTERNATIONAL SPORTS MOVEMENT, AND YOUR SPIRIT OF TRUE SPORTSMANSHIP TO-DAY WILL GIVE HOPE AND INSPIRATION TO THOUSANDS OF PARALYSED PEOPLE. NO GREATER CONTRIBUTION CAN BE MADE TO SOCIETY BY THE PARALYSED THAN TO HELP, THROUGH THE MEDIUM OF SPORT, TO FURTHER FRIENDSHIP AND UNDERSTANDING AMONGST NATIONS.
U.S. Para
By JOHN DOWN
It was one big merry-go-round Wednesday, second day of the Pan-Am Paraplegic Games.
Officials were running
Hamilton girl takes
Canada's first gold
g vorstellen.
der Beweis.
Rhein-Neckar
n direkt vor die Haus
d schwedische gelähmte Sportler gestern nach Heide

A Celebration
of Wheelchair Sports

So Get On With It

A Celebration of Wheelchair Sports

Marilee Weisman & Jan Godfrey

Doubleday Canada Limited
Toronto, Ontario

Doubleday & Company, Inc.
Garden City, New York

1976

ISBN: 0-385-12240-3
Library of Congress Catalog Card Number: 76-1458

Copyright © 1976 by Jan Godfrey and Marilee Weisman.
All rights reserved.

Design/Maher & Garbutt Ltd.
Printed and bound in Canada by
T. H. Best Printing Company Limited, Don Mills, Ontario

First Edition

" To me being in a chair is just like being any other man, doing what you have to to survive; working, driving, dating, doing whatever you want. I've tried not to let my chair stop me from doing what I want to do."

Julius Duval

Introduction *by Jan Godfrey*

Once you see the games and talk to the athletes, it gets into your blood. That's how it happened with Marilee, a free-lance writer who had researched disabled sports, written an article on the 1976 Olympiad for the Physically Disabled and then undertaken to interview and film the athletes participating in the 1975 International Stoke Mandeville Games.

It was her "getting to know" the athletes that brought this book about. She had talked to them, socialized with them and, most importantly, had been touched by them. She wanted to relate her experience to others. Then she approached me to help tell this story of disabled sports. Together we hope to communicate the meaning and the spirit of wheelchair sports to a wide audience.

The first time the idea of sports for the disabled was presented to me, I thought it must be a joke. But since I had been actively involved in sports before a car accident left me paralyzed from the waist down, I had the motivation needed to go out and determine what wheelchair sports were all about.

No one I knew had ever heard of, let alone participated in, wheelchair sports. We were curious, even keen, but none of us ever envisaged the seriousness of our training.

The next thing I knew, I'd been picked to represent Canada in track (60 meters) and field events (discus, javelin, shotput, club throw) at the paraplegic Pan American Games held in Winnipeg, Canada, in 1967. It was mind-boggling: 150 people whipping around the University of Manitoba campus in wheelchairs. And they were dead serious about competing. "What am I doing here?" I wondered.

The experience was incredible, but hardly prepared me for the stiff competition I encountered the following November at the paraplegic (Wheelchair) Olympic Games held in Tel Aviv, Israel. There were 30 nations and 750 competitors.

Comradeship and self-esteem were displayed by the athletes

everywhere, from the hush during the weightlifting in the gym to the warm and friendly smiles in the pub. Their spirit and keenness were overwhelming. For the first time it became clear to me that it was competition as tough as I'd known it before, and, yes, it was definitely out of my league.

These athletes had actually trained every day and undergone rigorous trials before they were selected to represent their countries at the international level. Most of them worked or went to school, leading normal lives in which training was just one more aspect of their daily routines. The proof of their dedication was shown by the records which fell daily.

To have been a part of this at the highest level of competition was extremely satisfying. And it still is, now that I think back. After all, how often in a lifetime does a person in or out of a wheelchair have the opportunity to witness such a degree of dedication and accomplishment?

Introduction *by Marilee Weisman*

When Dr. Stanley Schatz, Toronto neurosurgeon, came to her hospital room to talk about the future, Jan Godfrey was ready.

"You'll be in a wheelchair the rest of your life," he said. And Jan did one of her ruthlessly quick appraisals of the situation and told him (and herself) not to worry, that no matter what happened, she would never give up.

Since that day almost ten years ago, Jan has never given up. That chair that she rests in so easily it almost looks like fun often seems to disappear for all of us who know this lady. She represents quite neatly what it's all about. A career that is respectable and a full, active life that includes lots of gaiety, more than most able-bodied individuals seem to derive from their existence.

I had known Jan for a year before I went to visit her in her own apartment for the first time. We had lots to discuss regarding our book; ideas to share and argue about and finally resolve into viable entity. "Just a minute," I pleaded when I arrived there, "I have to phone my baby sitter."

There I stood daydreaming in the tiny alcove off the living room. A glance to the right and there was a perfectly normal washroom except that the usual wooden door had been replaced with pliable bamboo and beneath the usual towel rack was another, a mere foot and a half away from the floor.

Why this diminutive version, I wondered until I returned to the living room to find my co-author sitting in her *wheelchair*, asking me if I wanted a sherry.

Similar incidents were to happen again and again. I would often forget that Jan was in a chair.

Jan is Jan. And yes, the chair is a bit of a pain and if you're in it you have to put up with a lot of nonsense from people who think that it makes you different in any way that matters.

Well, it just doesn't matter. We all have to keep moving, in or out of chairs, with whatever disability we have. And *all* of us encounter some difficulties in our lives that we either rise above or let defeat us.

After all, Ed Membry, why bother to play golf when you're carrying a 25-pound load of steel brace on your left leg? And why, Doug Lyons, was it so important to break the world's shotput record? How about you, Jon Brown, you've never run a step in your life. What's driving you to push 561 pounds high into the air? Guts, spirit or simply powers of self-preservation?

These are some of the questions that Jan and I hope to answer in our book by means of pictures and words. Hopefully, they will be worthy of the talent they reveal.

A History of Wheelchair Sports

Sir Ludwig Guttmann

If you or I had sustained a spinal cord injury prior to World War II, our chances of surviving longer than three years would have been a meager 20 percent. Should it happen today, there would be an 80 percent likelihood of our living our full life expectancy. The reason for this dramatic change: the efforts and dedication of one man, Sir Ludwig Guttmann.

Born in Germany in 1899, Sir Ludwig qualified as a doctor in 1923, specializing in neurology and rising quickly to the top of his field. Within a decade he was renowned as one of Germany's best brain surgeons. But the 1930's brought with them sorrowful times for the Jewish population in Germany. After assisting many of his people to escape from the Nazis, Sir Ludwig fled from his homeland to the nation where he was to leave his mark on history.

England welcomed this distinguished doctor, at first offering him a post as research fellow in the Department of Neurosurgery, Oxford University, and then at the Peripheral Nerve Injury Unit, Wingfield Moris Orthopaedic Hospital, Oxford.

In 1944 the British government asked him to set up a spinal injuries unit at Stoke Mandeville Hospital, Aylesbury, to care for the large number of war-wounded veterans. On February 1, 1944, the center opened.

"When I first arrived at Stoke, those with spinal cord injuries were thought of as hopeless cripples," Sir Ludwig recalls. Bladder and subsequent kidney malfunction as well as infected bed sores were considered inevitable complications. "I did not accept this defeatist attitude. My philosophy was that these complications could not only be controlled but altogether avoided."

He was also aware of another problem: "Paralyzed individuals lose self-confidence and activity of mind and personal dignity. They become encapsulated and anti-social."

Sir Ludwig set up a new program of treatment that was designed not only to prolong life but to help the disabled patients to overcome their psychological difficulties and to become useful and respected members of society. Sport, he believed, would encourage them to make the most of their remaining physical capabilities, provide much-needed exercise and restore mental equilibrium. He introduced a few games—darts, archery, snooker and table tennis—and soon followed up with team sports like wheelchair polo and basketball. Hospital life was no longer restricted and boring. As one patient put it: "We're so busy in this bloody place we haven't got time to be ill."

The therapeutic value of the program soon became evident, and as the patients regained strength, coordination, and confidence they began to find regular work and a place in the outside world.

A milestone event took place on July 28, 1948, when 16 paralyzed British ex-servicemen and women engaged in an archery competition on the fields of Stoke. This was the first of the Stoke Mandeville Games, now an annual event.

"That day also saw the opening ceremony of the 1948 Olympic games in London," Sir Ludwig says. "The coincidence gave me an idea which I voiced at the 1949 Stoke Mandeville Games. Looking into the future, I prophesied that the time would come when this new sports event of ours would be truly international and the Stoke Mandeville Games would achieve world fame as the disabled person's equivalent of the Olympics."

International Games

The concept of sports for the physically disabled spread to other countries, and year by year the numbers of sports and participants increased. In 1952 the international aspect of Sir Ludwig's dream became a reality when a small team of ex-servicemen from the Netherlands came to Stoke Mandeville. The International Stoke Mandeville Games (I.S.M.G.) now ranks as one of the most important for wheelchair athletes. It is the only annual competition that welcomes teams from all parts of the world. These men and women have the opportunity to travel, participate in demanding games that are conducted according to international rules and meet in comradeship with their peers.

In 1956 the Fearnley Cup, an Olympic award for outstanding achievement in the service of the Olympic ideal, was presented to the Stoke Mandeville Games by the Olympic Committee during the Melbourne Games. This marked the first time that disabled athletes had won such an honour.

Over the years various offshoots sprang from the original I.S.M.G. In 1962 the first British Commonwealth Games were held in Perth, Australia, and continued every four years up to and including 1974 in New Zealand, after which they were disbanded due to lack of funds.

The Pan American Games started in Winnipeg, Canada, in 1967, with Argentina, Trinidad and Tobago, Jamaica, Mexico, Peru, the United States and Canada participating in that competition. The Pan American Games Council has sought to develop sports in North, Central and South America. These games are held every two years.

When the British Commonwealth games ended, the Far Eastern and South Pacific Games (F.E.S.P.I.C.) were started, the first being held in Osaka, Japan. This event was heralded as the eastern version of the Pan American Games, giving even more countries an opportunity to compete and to further develop sports for the disabled.

In 1960 the games for the disabled were held in Italy, the country of the regular Olympics, under Olympic rules and in an Olympic stadium. The existing facilities were used. This created problems, as the top-of-the-mountain setting necessitated the daily carrying of each athlete up and down the hill.

It was after these games that Sir Ludwig stood on the papal balcony beside Pope John XXIII while His Holiness praised the 400 paralyzed athletes assembled below: "The weakening of your physical powers has not impaired your eagerness and in these recent days you have taken part in all kinds of games, the practice of which must have seemed forever impossible.

"You have given a great example, which we would like to emphasize because it can be a lead to everyone. You have shown what an energetic soul can achieve in spite of apparently insurmountable obstacles imposed by the body. You are the living demonstration of the marvels of the virtue of energy."

The success of the Rome Olympics inspired the Stoke Mandeville Games Committee to plan to hold Olympic year games every fourth year, and in the country of the regular competitions whenever possible. An Olympic year is thus the only one in which the international games are not held at Stoke Mandeville.

The 1964 Olympics for wheelchair athletes were held in Tokyo, Japan. And this was just two years after only two competitors represented Japan at the I.S.M.G. Organizers always hope that the games will make the public aware of the potential of the disabled members within society and that long-term benefits will follow. In Japan, after and due to the '64 disabled Olympics, the Ministry of Labor built two factories for paralyzed and other severely handicapped individuals.

Tel Aviv, Israel, was the site of the 1968 disabled Olympics and in 1972 Heidelberg, Germany, was the host city. Etobicoke (Toronto), Canada, was chosen as the locale for the 1976 Olympics — with 1,000 wheelchair, 300 blind and 300 amputee athletes from more than 60 countries competing. All this less than two decades after those 16 men and women shot bows and arrows on the lawn at Stoke Mandeville.

Canada

Canada's unofficial beginnings included such local activities as the competitions held in June, 1947, at Deer Lodge Hospital, Manitoba, involving archery, milk bottle pitching, basketball throw, ring toss, croquet and golf putting. For almost 20 years wheelchair sports continued on an informal basis, lacking organization and public recognition. It took a coincidence of time, place and person to spur Canada's official appearance on the international scene.

As orthopedic consultant to the Canadian Olympic team in Tokyo, Japan, in 1964, Dr. Robert W. Jackson had the opportunity to witness the games for the disabled that occurred after the regular event. He noted the absence of any Canadian participants and promised Sir Ludwig Guttman that Canada would be represented at the games four years later. That promise was kept: at Tel Aviv in 1968, Canada fielded 22 athletes, her first Olympic team.

When he returned home in 1965, Dr. Jackson began talking about the sports achievements he had observed. From a modest beginning of eight people practicing field events one Saturday at Varsity Stadium, Toronto, the Coasters Athletic Club was formed in May 1967.

While Dr. Jackson was stirring up interest in Ontario, June Wilson, a physiotherapist in Winnipeg, persuaded Ben Reimer to compete in Kingston, Jamaica, at the 1966 British Commonwealth Games. He was the only Canadian present. Furthermore, in August, 1967, it was Winnipeg that hosted the first Pan American Games for disabled athletes. Dr. Jackson's Coasters Club placed 13 members on the Canadian team; these athletes acquired 21 medals for their efforts.

"A lot of people tend to think of wheelchair sports as a freak show," says Dr. Jackson, "but what they do see is tough competition between people who are entirely normal except for their inability to walk."

1967 also marked the formation of the Canadian Wheelchair Sports Association, which Dr. Jackson chaired for the next six years. He then resigned to devote his energies to the 1976 Olympiad.

United States

American involvement in wheelchair sports deserves mention, so exceptional are the motivation and the talent of the U.S. athletes. In 1946 wheelchair basketball was merely a pastime when a bunch of players of the sport (World War II veterans), aptly called the Flying Wheels, of Van Nuys, California, toured the United States playing exhibition games against local teams. This sparked interest and enthusiasm not only among potential wheelchair athletes but in the general community as well. At this point two men emerged who remain key figures in wheelchair sports in their country.

Ben Lipton had been taught from an early age that "it wasn't good enough to just *take* in life, one had to give something back." First, while a part of the Army Medical Corps, he trained others to work with the disabled. Then he became a liaison between the Veterans' Administration and various areas of work and education. Soon he was Director of the Bulova School of Watchmaking, a tuition-free school for the disabled in New York. Meanwhile he was assisting in the organization, coaching and development of wheelchair sports on the local as well as the national level.

In 1946 Mr. Lipton, along with Tim Nugent, Director of Student Rehabilitation at the University of Illinois and coach of the Illinois Gizz Kids Basketball team, worked to develop wheelchair tournaments in that sport. Mr. Nugent organized the first national basketball games, and teams came from all over the United States. Now the U.S. boasts one of the top international teams in sports for the disabled: a band of superstars.

Financial Support

Competing costs money. Where do the funds come from? In Canada, government, private companies and individuals are asked to contribute. The same holds true for Great Britain, where Sir Ludwig's powers of persuasion have been known to reap great financial support for his athletes. In the United States money comes entirely from private sources.

If money is a problem in these large countries, it is not hard to imagine how difficult it is for smaller nations to support their athletes. When a team is sent to an international event, room, board and some sightseeing excursions are paid for by the host nation. But there remain air fare, cost of equipment and uniforms and all the incidental expenses incurred by any traveler to another country. Yet each year a new nation manages to appear, usually through the efforts of one or two dedicated individuals.

The Future

The ultimate goal of wheelchair sports is a change in attitude: first in the psyche of the athlete who will be able to view himself with healthy respect in the light of his effort and accomplishments, and secondly in the collective mind of the public.

Dr. Robert W. Jackson says, "Perhaps when an employer sees the high level of performance at the games, when he sees an athlete in a chair race a six-minute mile or do a heavyweight bench press of 600 pounds, then he may realize that such an individual can come to work and put in an eight-hour day. Then he'll truly be able to accept the maxim that it's ability and not disability that counts."

Sir Ludwig Guttmann *(second from right).*

Contents

A Celebration
of Wheelchair Sports

PART ONE

To Be Mobile...

"One day you are running around and the next day you are on your back. And when you look in the mirror you suddenly realize it's you in that condition."

Jan Godfrey

"I came home knowing that it was up to me: I was either going to live or die in the fullest sense of those words. I came to believe that in spite of my paralysis I could make my time worthwhile. I decided not to let my life dribble down the drain." *Tony Bagnato*

"When people first see me in a wheelchair, they expect me either to fall out, throw up or babble incoherently. They're amazed when I do none of these."

Doug Mowat

"We've made almost everything from intersections to public buildings practically inaccessible. After all, it's not that the disabled are asking for anything special. They'd just like to enjoy some of the things the rest of us take for granted — like a trip to the corner store."
Canadian Rehabilitation Council for the Disabled.

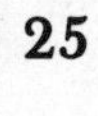

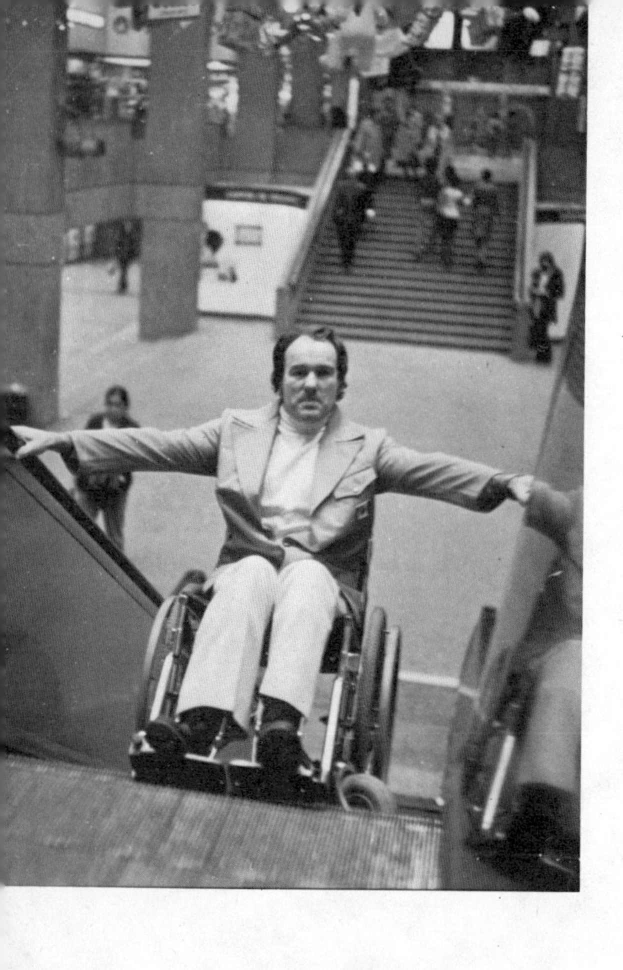

This telephone is placed close enough to the ground to be reached by someone in a wheelchair.

Much is said about how society should change to make life easier for the disabled. Ramping of all public buildings or complete redesign of a transit system are among the many demands.

At the very least, wheelchairs should be taken into consideration at the planning stage of new buildings. It is estimated that this would add only 1 percent to the final cost. Even if only one out of every seven people is disabled, it is wise to make places accessible. If it's easy for someone in a wheelchair, then it's good for everybody and particularly beneficial for those with heart disease, respiratory ailments or any serious physical problem. We will all grow old one day, and accessible buildings, streets, and subways will then function to our advantage as well.

"A person in a wheelchair is open to social difficulties not only because his disability places physical limitations on him but more importantly because it is visible and can not be masked. And if it's visible, then it's observable, obviously different." *Marilee Weisman*

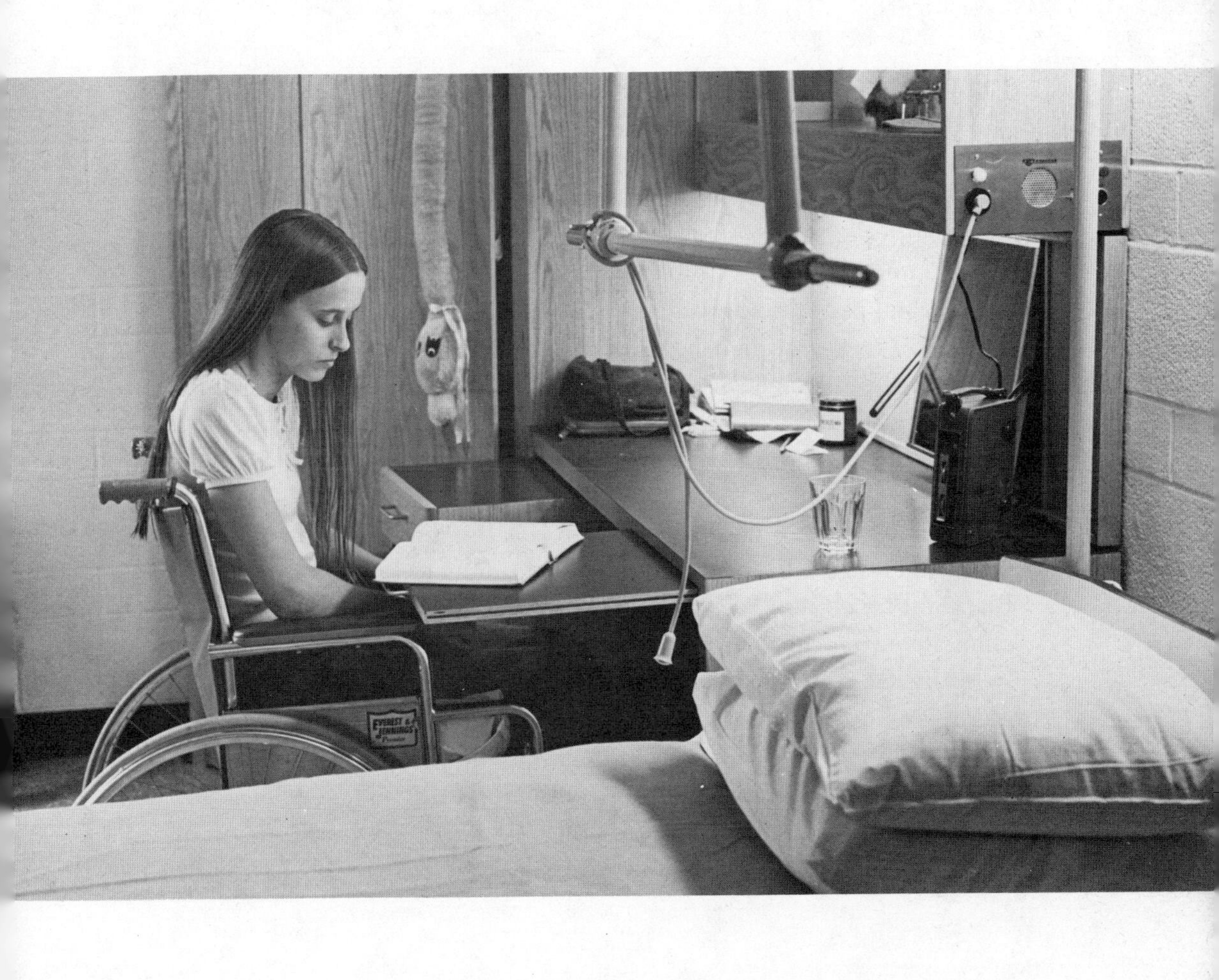
EVEREST &
JENNINGS

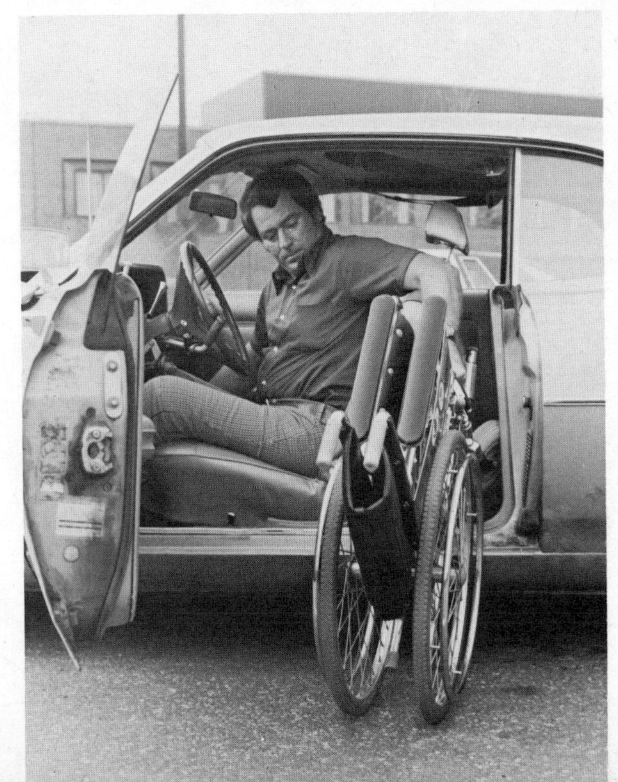

Rehabilitation favors the athletic person because he or she is physically more adept and therefore able to become independent more rapidly than those less fit. Even handling a chair comes more easily to the formerly active individual. And the sooner the person in a chair can become reasonably independent, the better it is for his self-image.

An ideal program helps the paralyzed individual to achieve for himself. The situation at a rehabilitation center should be realistic. There will be, of necessity, certain appropriate modifications for large numbers of patients in wheelchairs, but these adjustments have to be tempered with some features that will be found outside this sheltered environment.

It is easy to use a washroom when it is ten feet by ten feet or to press an elevator button placed only three feet above floor level. But sometime before facing the outside world there should be a chance to attempt the difficulties that will be encountered there.

Many rehabilitation centers recognize this need and have set up "halfway houses" as a preliminary step to discharge into society. With that brief stage mastered, the chair-bound person can move out to face all the challenges of his new status.

Hans Rosenhast gets together with some friends.

Ben Lipton *(seated at table)* chairs a meeting of the U.S. National Wheelchair Sports Association.

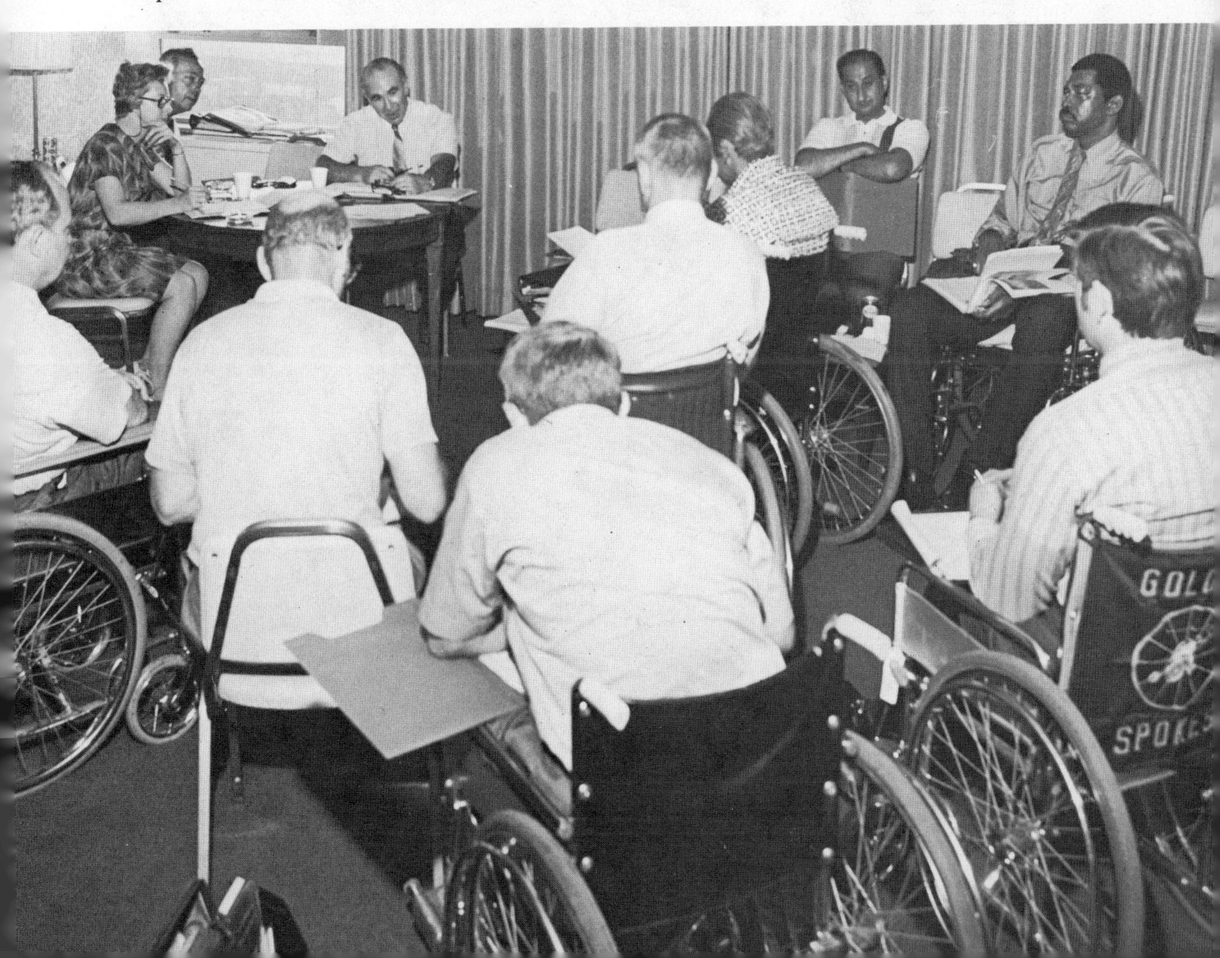

"Though people in wheelchairs seem isolated, they want social contact; though they must modify their sexual activity, they are not bereft of sexuality; though they need your understanding and assistance, they reject your pity and over-protection." *Marilee Weisman*

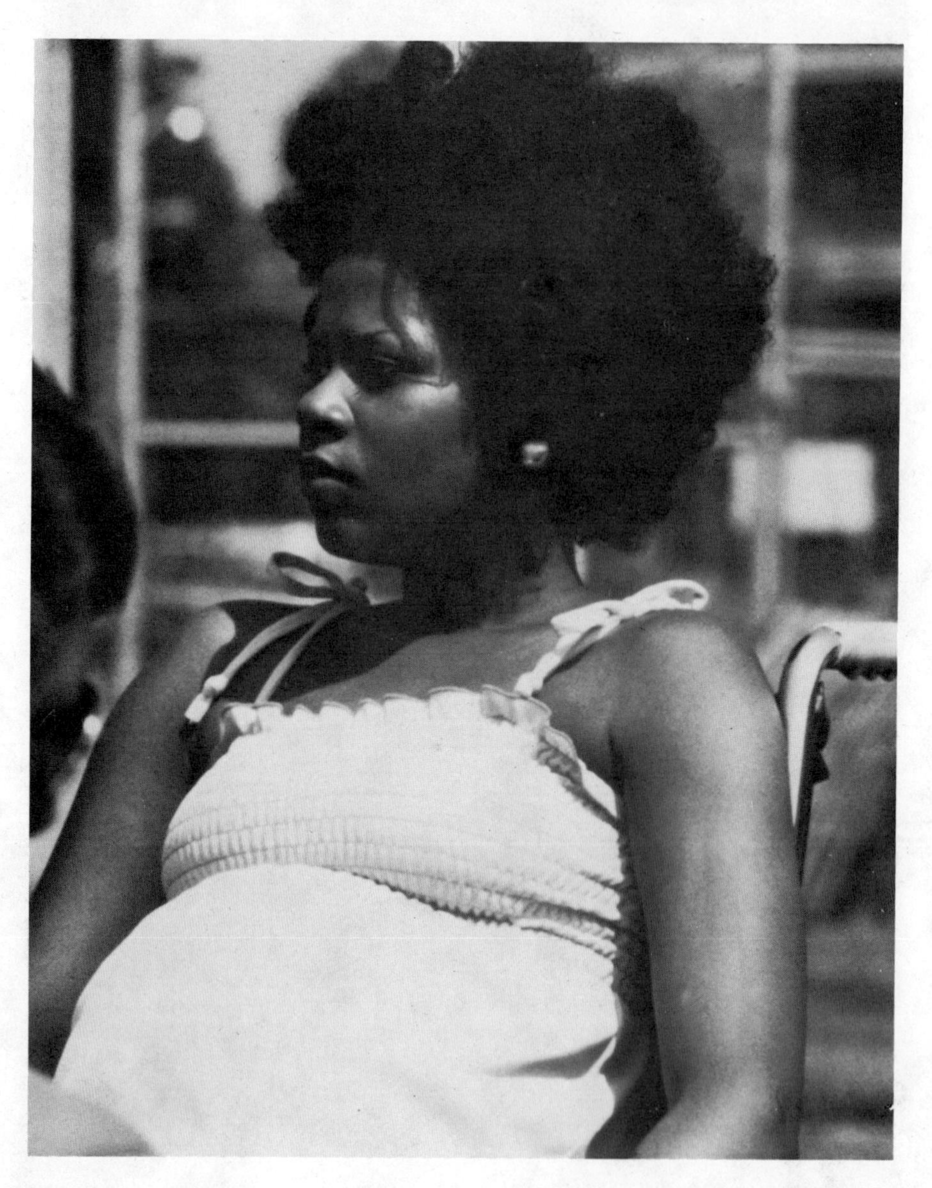

Doug and Marnie Bovee shortly after their marriage. They both competed in the 1971 International Stoke Mandeville Games.

"If a person with a severe disability has gone on to live his life effectively, then one hour after you meet him, you should forget he's in a wheelchair. If you still see or feel the chair, then usually the fault lies with the paraplegic." *Doug Wilson*

Diane Crowe dances with Roger Campbell, a former Canadian coach, at the Paralympic Sports Association's annual dinner. Diane is a physical education graduate from the University of Alberta: "I didn't just want to be a secretary. I took a business course and didn't like it. A while ago, when I was practice teaching at a rehabilitation center, I found the kids could really relate to me. I can push them harder because I'm in a chair and I can do it."

Ed Membry contracted polio when he was seven. "Sure, I said, 'Why me?' when I got polio even though I was just a kid. But I passed through that and now I do everything."

Ed remains in a wheelchair during working hours but on the golf course he manages with a cart and his two canes.

It is not easy to climb out of a sand trap, but the excellent wedge shot that Ed just hit makes it worthwhile.

"You soon become accustomed to the new gear you are sporting and slowly you realize that the 'new' me is just an extension of the 'old' me." *Jan Godfrey*

"Stage one was easy. I felt like a little boy with the measles or the flu. People came to visit me in hospital bearing presents. I was the center of attention: it was great.

"I also believed that one day I would get up, when I got tired of this game, and go back to being an ordinary person.

"Then I grew to realize that my situation was permanent and the grieving period began. I grieved for the loss of abilities . . . emotive things like running into the sea with my kids, going to places that are inaccessible to wheelchairs, like the top of a cliff, looking out at the view I had loved so much.

"And I haven't stopped grieving yet."

Dr. Eifion Owens

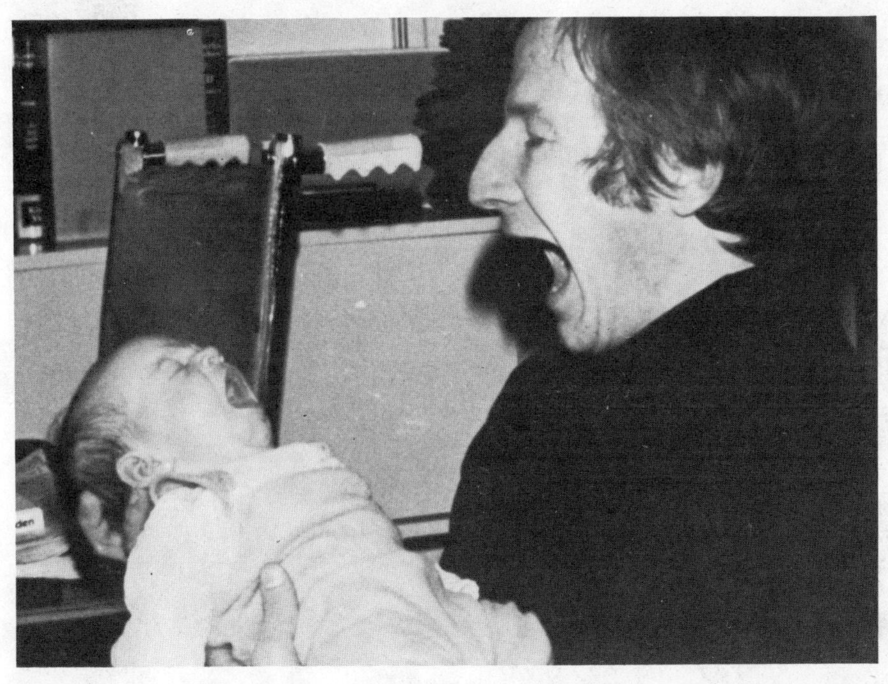

Jurg Rickert, a Swiss, with his son. Jurg has been a paraplegic since 1967.

It is still possible to fully share some activities.

Group Captain Douglas Bader, legless flying ace from World War II, pays his annual visit to the I.S.M.G. (1975) and Sir Ludwig Guttman (left foreground) and Dr. Robert W. Jackson (right rear).

"The accident in which I lost my legs was entirely my fault and I think it makes an enormous difference to one's approach to disability if you've done it yourself.

"One says, 'You were to blame, old boy, and nobody else, so get on from there.'

"You don't want sympathy. You don't want pity. All you want is for other people to allow you to conduct your life.

"Obviously you need some help. If you're in a wheelchair, you can't climb 555 steps to get to the top of Notre Dame, so somebody can push you up, someone can help you. You can ask for that." *Douglas Bader*

"When you're in a wheelchair people tend to look at the chair and not the man in it. So every time you meet somebody new you have to prove you're a man. But I don't feel I have to prove I'm a man, I know I'm one." Julius Duval.

PART TWO

Sports

"Wheelchair sports involve a minimum of adaptation for the disabled individual. The same is true of everyday life: a disabled individual requires of society only a few adaptations so that he can function." *Marilee Weisman*

"To show my appreciation, I try to do my best in these games." *Delores Mullings*

"From a physical point of view, sport is of immense therapeutic value. It is the most natural form of remedial exercise and can be used successfully as a complement to the conventional methods of physiotherapy." *Sir Ludwig Guttmann*

"I didn't accomplish too much in life before I got hurt, but things changed a lot after it happened.

"I know this might sound a bit strange, but personally, it was good for me." *Brian Halliday*

"While physiotherapy is work; sport is fun . . . participation in sport gives our people a new lease on life. Pretty soon, they discover they are useful, productive citizens again." *Dr. Robert W. Jackson*

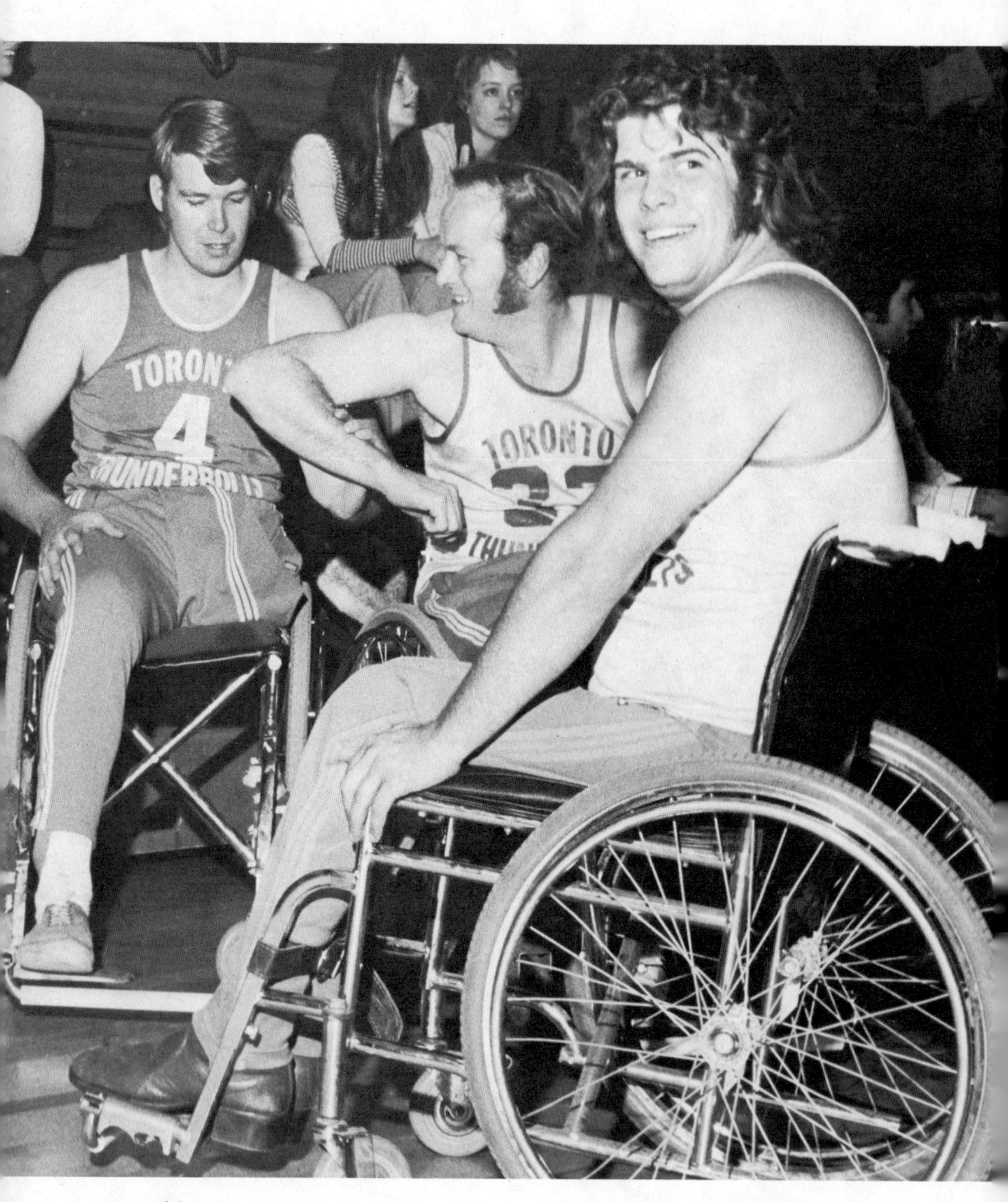
4
TORONTO

To ensure fair competition between disabled athletes, a method of classification has been devised by officials of wheelchair sports. Upon arriving at international games all participants must undergo extensive medical examinations by a committee of doctors for this purpose. Classes are numbered from 1 to 6—the *lower* the number, the *more severely disabled.* Class 1 is divided further into 1A, 1B and 1C: all athletes in this division are quadriplegic. Gold, silver and bronze medals are awarded to first-, second- and third-place winners in each class in all sports.

Each competitor may enter a maximum of eight events (excluding team events). Each different stroke in swimming, each implement in field events and each weapon in fencing count as one event.

Occasionally, competitors enter an event in a class lower than their own (less disabled competition) and do remarkably well. For example, Tommy Hite of Florida holds the world record in the 60-meter dash both in his Class 1B and also in Class 1C.

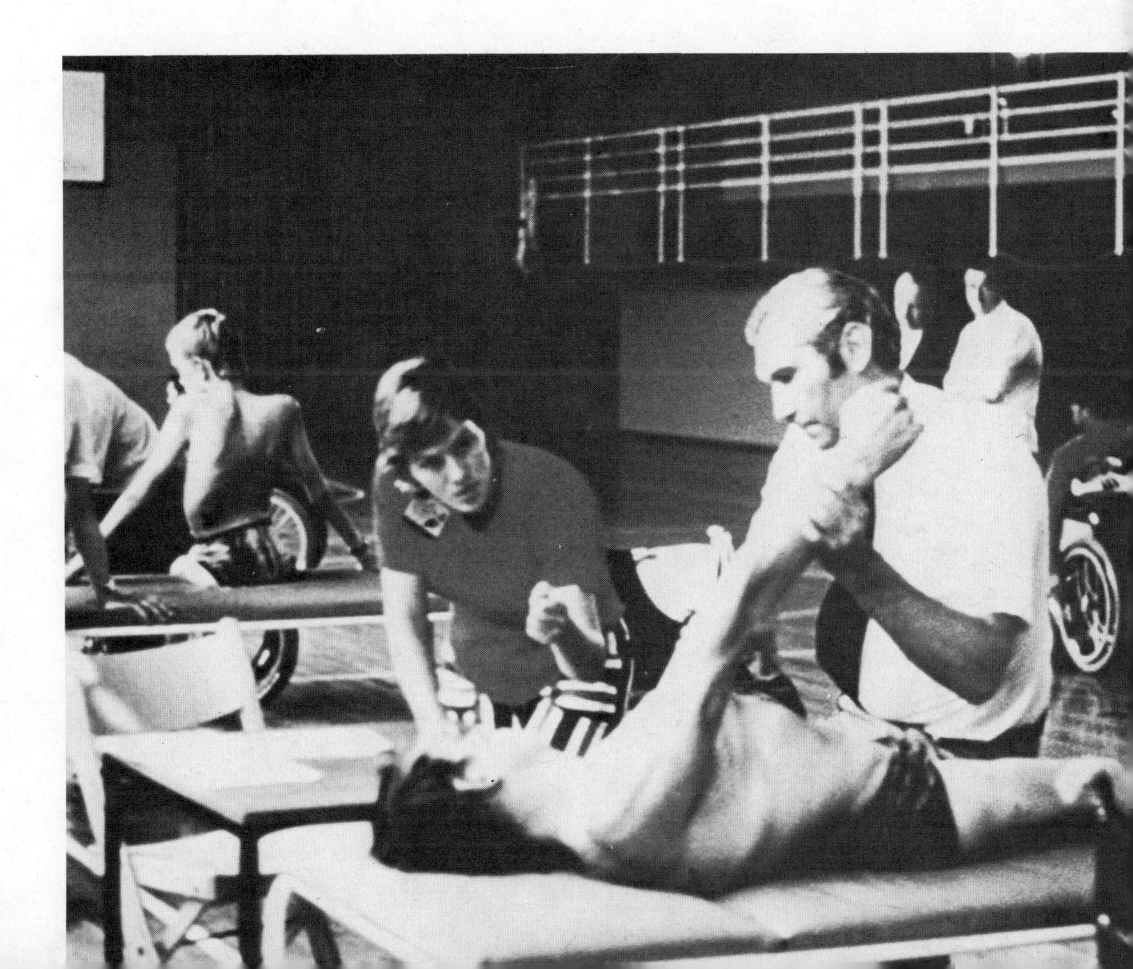

Medical Terms

Paraplegia: paralysis of the lower extremities and more or less of the trunk.

Quadriplegia: sometimes referred to as tetraplegia; paralysis which involves not only the lower limbs but affects the upper ones to varying degrees.

Paralysis in both instances affects motor function, circulation and to some extent bladder and bowel control.

Paralysis can occur as a result of accidents in which there is complete or partial severance of the spinal cord, with paralysis from the site of the injury down. Diseases, such as polio, can also cause paralysis. Many of the top disabled athletes around the world were victims of a series of outbreaks of poliomyelitis in the 1950's.

Post-polio athletes have one major advantage over traumatically injured competitors: they retain most sensation in their bodies. This sometimes enables them to navigate on foot, with the aid of braces and crutches, a feat much more difficult for those who have suffered trauma.

Opening Ceremonies

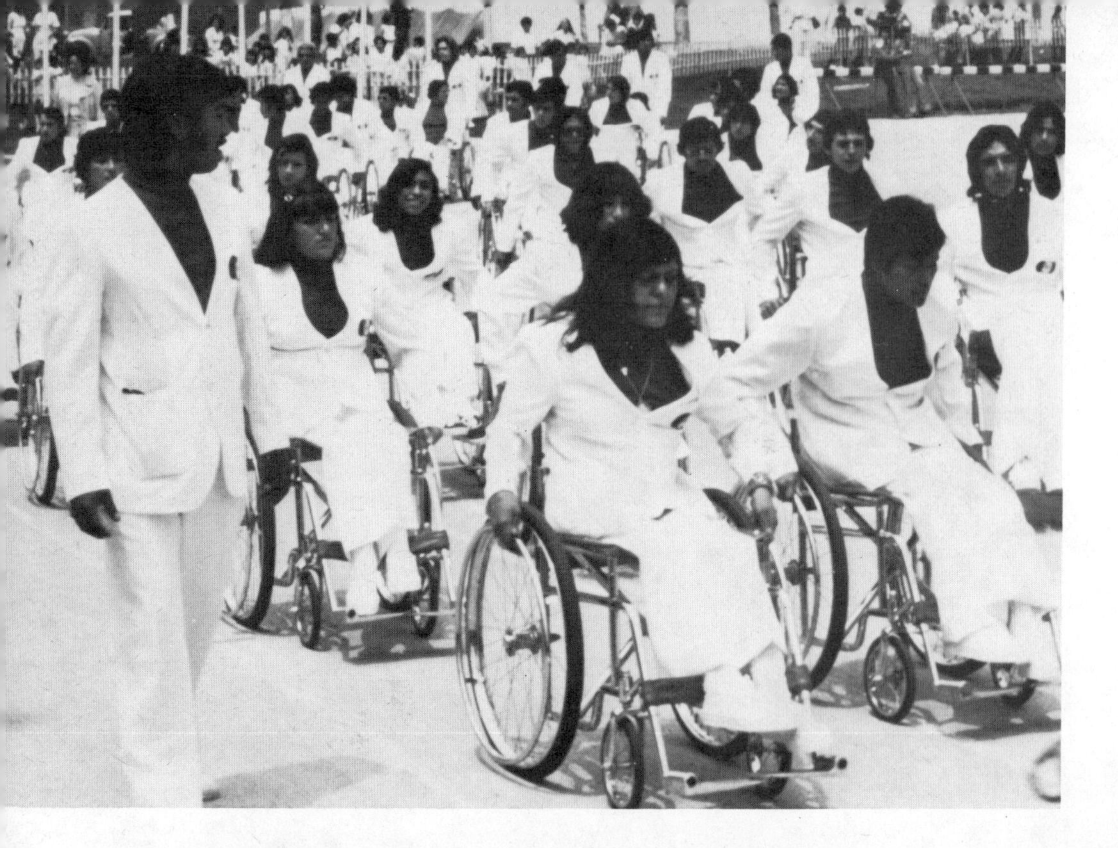

Basketball

Basketball, the only team sport played at the wheelchair Olympics, is one of the oldest and most popular of all wheelchair sports. It is also the roughest. Players are bumped into and tossed from their chairs. If they're not in danger, play continues. The final basketball game, which is usually played the afternoon of the last day of international competition, invariably features a fiercely fought battle between Israel and the United States.

In many areas, because of the lack of disabled people, house leagues have formed utilizing able-bodied players in wheelchairs. Many blisters and tumbles are evident when someone not used to handling a chair attempts to play a complete game of basketball.

The Harlem Globetrotters, in wheelchairs, once played a handicapped team. They lost.

Rules have been only slightly modified for wheelchair competitors. The basket is set at regulation height of ten feet. The ball is placed on the lap and the athlete can take two pushes of his wheelchair; then he must dribble or be called for traveling, although a player can coast an unlimited distance. Fouls are called similarly to regular basketball. The wheelchair's front wheels must be behind the free throw line before taking a penalty shot. A player is allowed five seconds in the key, only two seconds more than able-bodied athletes.

To ensure that no side fields a team far superior in terms of degree of disability, each player is assigned a point value according to his classification (see Classification, page 45). The most disabled classes, namely 1, 2 and 3, are all assigned one point. Class 4 rates two points and Class 5 three points. A fielded team must not collectively exceed 11 points.

The backs of these chairs have been cut down to give the players greater range of movement.

"It is no exaggeration to say that the paraplegic and his chair have become one, in the same way as a first-class horseman and his mount." *Sir Ludwig Guttmann*

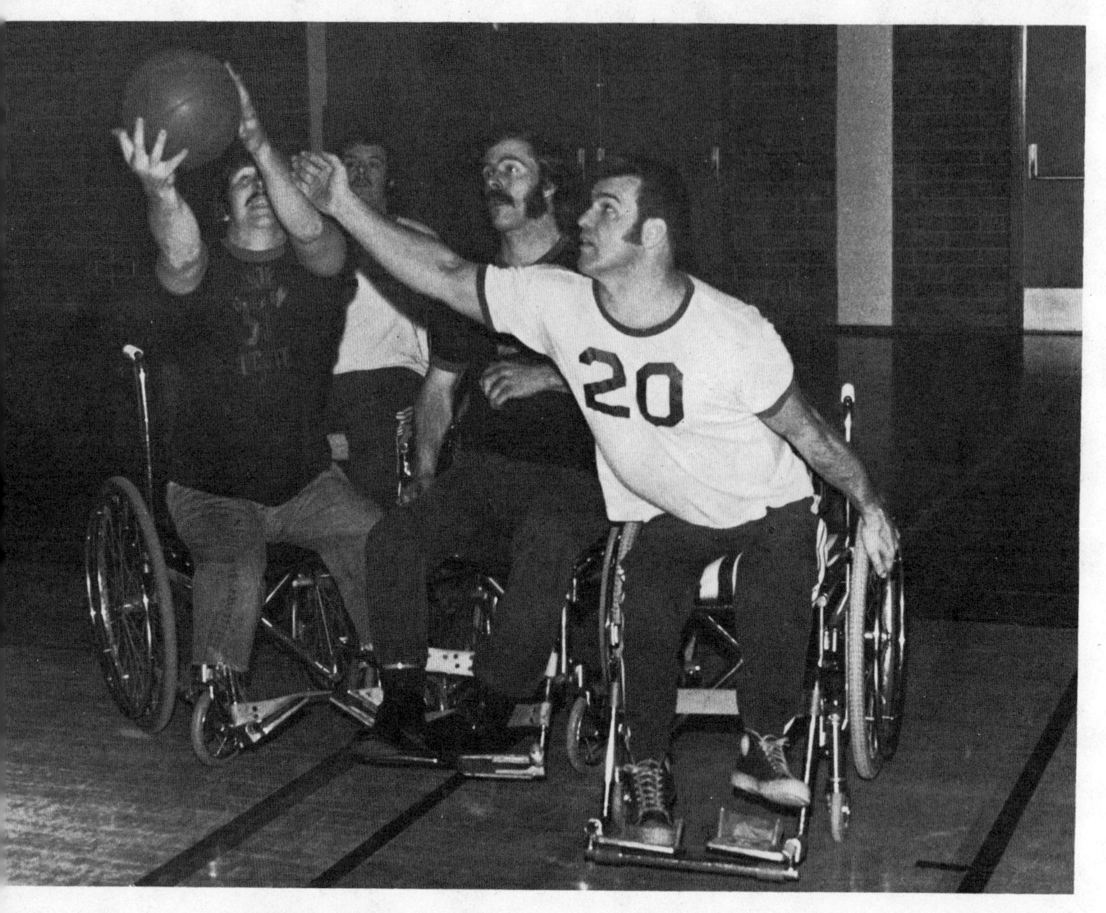

Canadian Eugene Reimer, No. 20, contracted polio at age four. He is married with three children. "I remember wearing braces on both legs during my childhood. I suppose in some ways I am luckier than others because I can't remember what it was like to run.

"Until 1967, when sport became recognized as therapy, I was locked out of participation. Now I'm part of something I've always loved."

Time stops just long enough for a player to return to his chair.

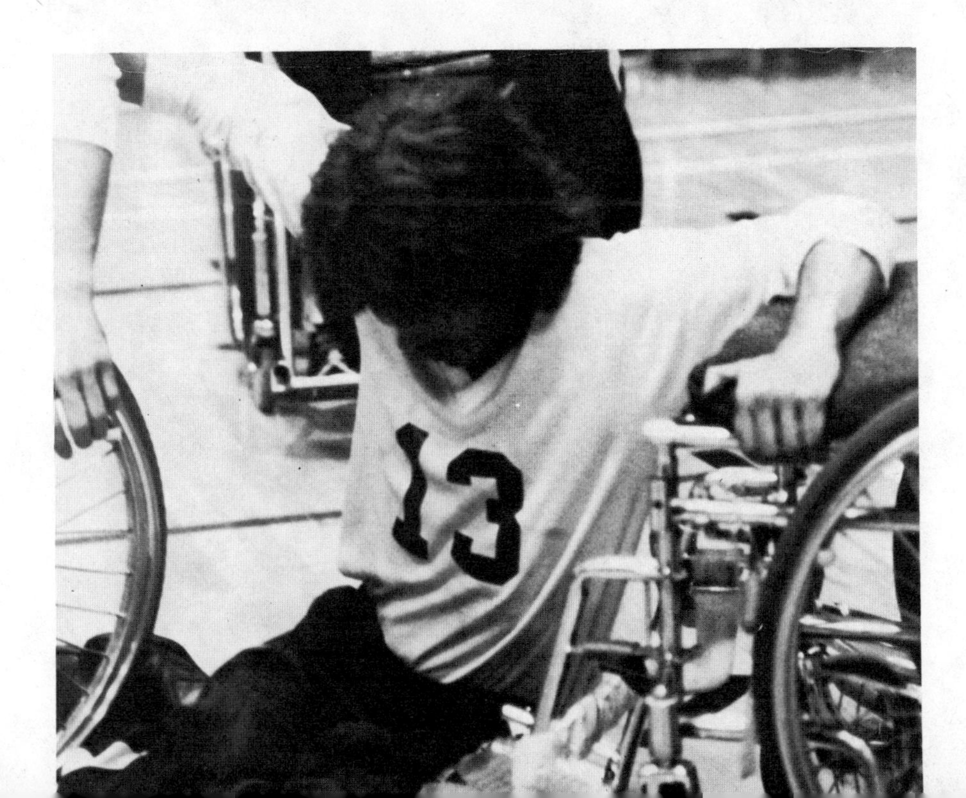

Portugal's first basketball team (1970).

Jamaica meets Argentina during the 1973 Pan American Games in Lima, Peru.

The final game (Argentina, 1972)

Archery

The area surrounding the archery event has a stillness about it unlike that for any other competition.

It is one of the few sports in which disabled and able-bodied athletes can compete on equal terms. Archery follows the same rules used in the able-bodied version, established by the international archery association known as F.I.T.A. although splints may be used by severely disabled quadriplegics to maintain stability of their wrists. All archers *must* shoot from their wheelchairs.

Archery tests not only skill but also endurance—competition runs for several continuous hours in the day.

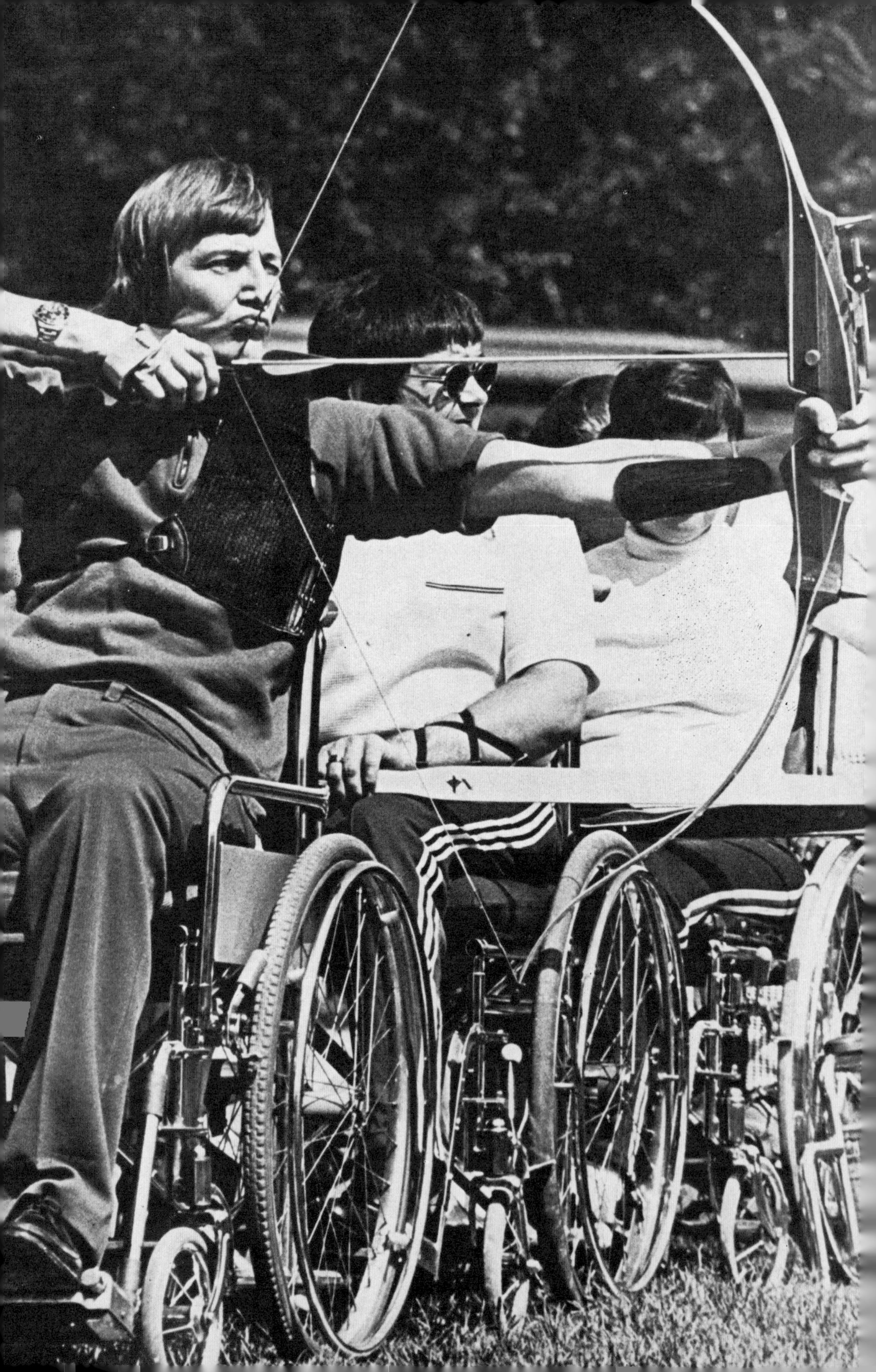

Tom Parker of Vancouver, British Columbia, is a quadriplegic who captured the gold medal in the archery competition at Stoke Mandeville in 1975, setting a new world record.

Brian Ward, Class 3.

Bruce Karr, 35 years old and a post-polio paraplegic, is a senior buyer for United Airlines.

Congratulations from his daughter.

Irene Miller of Canada.

Archers take aim in Solo, Indonesia.

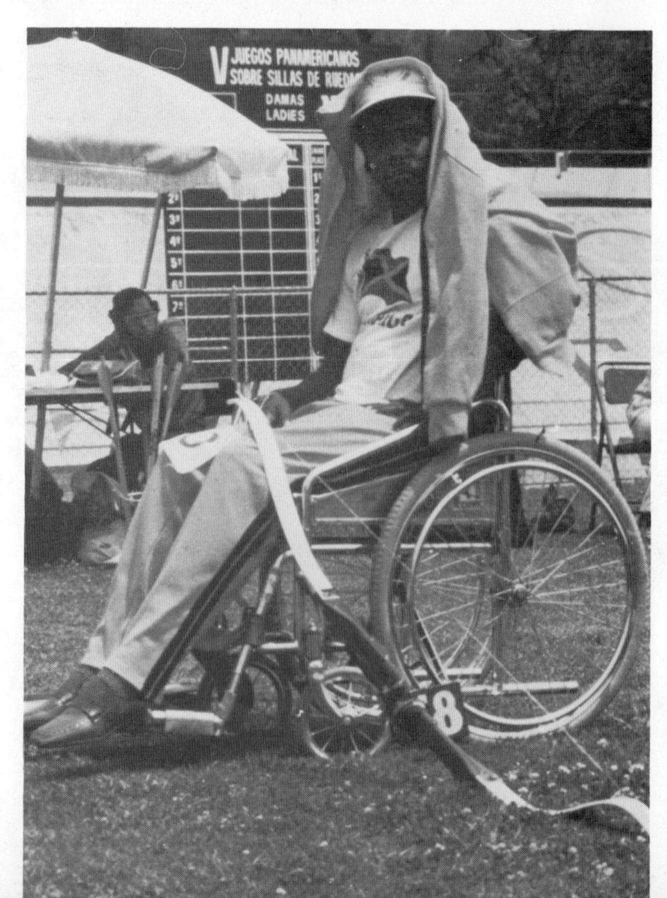

Dartchery

Dartchery has one major advantage over archery. Since it uses a target set only 15 feet from the shooter, it can more easily be practiced indoors. Unlike archery, this is a sport played only by wheelchair athletes.

Dartchery rules are similar to those for darts, but archery bow and arrows are used.

Swimming

Swimming is often the first physical activity of any duration open to the newly disabled person. The buoyant properties of water allow the use of muscles which, under ordinary circumstances, are too weak to be moved. In water the disabled person can lose, for a while, much of the feeling of paralysis.

At the games, swimming events are ordinarily contested by a particularly dedicated group of athletes. In many cases this is the only sport in which they participate. In competition the major difficulties occur at the start and turns of a race.

Swimming is not only a fiercely contested Olympic sport but one of the most popular and effective forms of therapy. Many people continue to swim regularly long after they have stopped competing at the local, national and international levels.

Swimming prowess is not limited to competition. In the summer of 1975 John Robertson, an American paraplegic, came within a half-mile of swimming the English Channel.

Above all, swimming enables the paralyzed person to independently move about, free of the ever-present wheelchair.

Stan Stronge, a rehabilitation counselor and former competitor from British Columbia, gives his swimmers some helpful hints.

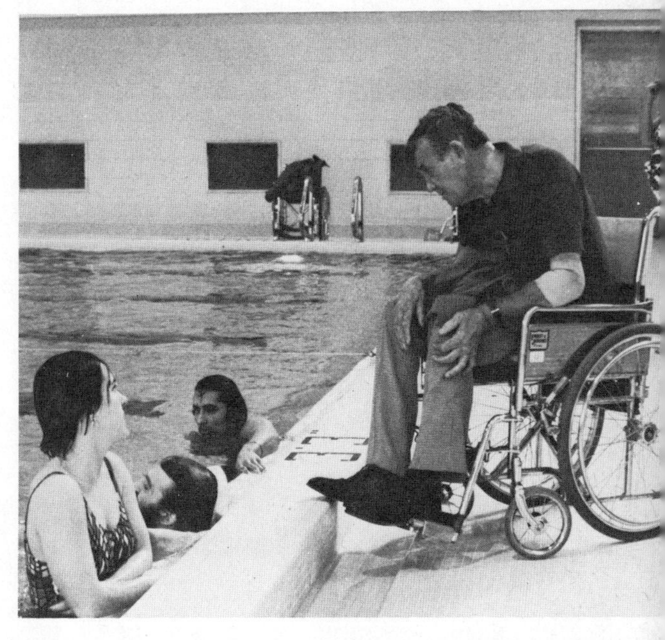

The paraplegic swimmer must tow the added burden of weighty limbs.

"Many people naturally feel a great deal of bitterness when they lose the use of their legs or arms or both, and competitions like this seem to give them a way of working some of this out." *Reg Muise*

Sarah Newland of Kingston, Jamaica *(center of picture)*, is seen during a practice session with two American athletes. The occasion was the fourth annual Pan American Games in Lima, Peru, 1973. Sarah won three gold medals for swimming and a silver for basketball.

In 1965 Sarah swam three miles in open sea—the annual cross-harbor race—as the only handicapped participant. She placed fifth among the ladies and was faster than some of the men, with a time of 1:11:43. In recognition of this accomplishment Sarah was awarded Jamaica's Sportswoman of the Year title for 1965.

LIBRARY
OF
MOUNT ST. MARY'S
COLLEGE
EMMITSBURG, MARYLAND

The backstroke: an arm is lifted gracefully from the water in swanlike motion.

The buoyancy of water is physically very pleasurable. And, if the disabled swimmer masters this element, he or she is free to pursue other activities with safety: sailing, fishing and waterskiing.

Field Events

Field events consist of shotput, javelin, precision javelin, discus and club throw. Precision javelin tests accuracy rather than distance: the winner places the most javelins closest to the center of a designated target area. Generally, a specialist in one field event takes part in all the others. Occasionally, one person will excel in several events, as does Tommy Hite of the U.S.A. He holds records in shotput, discus and club throw.

A raised semicircular band of metal marks the "throwing circle." The wheelchair must remain inside this circle; otherwise the throw is disqualified. The athlete's feet must not touch the ground before the throw is completed. Where muscle spasm is a medically certifiable problem, straps are allowed.

The wheelchair is secured in place within the throwing circle by an approved holding device. Or else a coach or heavy friend may hold on to the back of the chair to secure it in place. During the competition, this "anchor" often appears to be straining as much as the actual contestant.

After completing the three required throws the competitor must leave by the back of the circle.

Shotput

Doug Lyons prepares for a record-breaking shotput throw of 26 feet at Stoke Mandeville, July, 1975. A former policeman from Drummondville, Quebec, Doug was shot in the back while answering a robbery call in 1970. On November 28, 1975, he was named the top Quebec amateur athlete of the year, winning over four able-bodied opponents. Says Doug, "this finally puts handicapped sports on the same level as regular sport. Never again will we be treated as children playing."

"The games are a tremendous thing. When you are first in a chair you think 'this is the end,' but when you suddenly have a chance to be an athlete again . . . that's really something." Reg Muise, Class 1B.

American athlete Julius Duval putting the shot. This is just one of the many sports this man has mastered. At present Julius holds world records for the shotput, discus and as part of a relay team.

Lucy Raiche of Nova Scotia developed the strength to put the shot by her determined walk with braces and crutches 1½ miles to basketball practice.

uth Rosenbaum of Hempstead, New York.

Discus

"All athletes try to gain that extra edge. With some, it's the type of track shoes they wear, with me it's my wheelchair." *Eugene Reimer*

The cutaway wheelchair is for greater range of motion, and the blocks under this Israeli girl's feet are for stability.

Diane Crowe of Edmonton, Alberta, displays gold medal form at the British Columbia National Games in June, 1973. This effort went 39 feet, 8 inches. In 1963, at the age of 15, Diane was injured in a car accident. Six years later she was an active participant in wheelchair sports. "Much aggression is released through training. I am better able to accept my disability as well as those of others . . ."

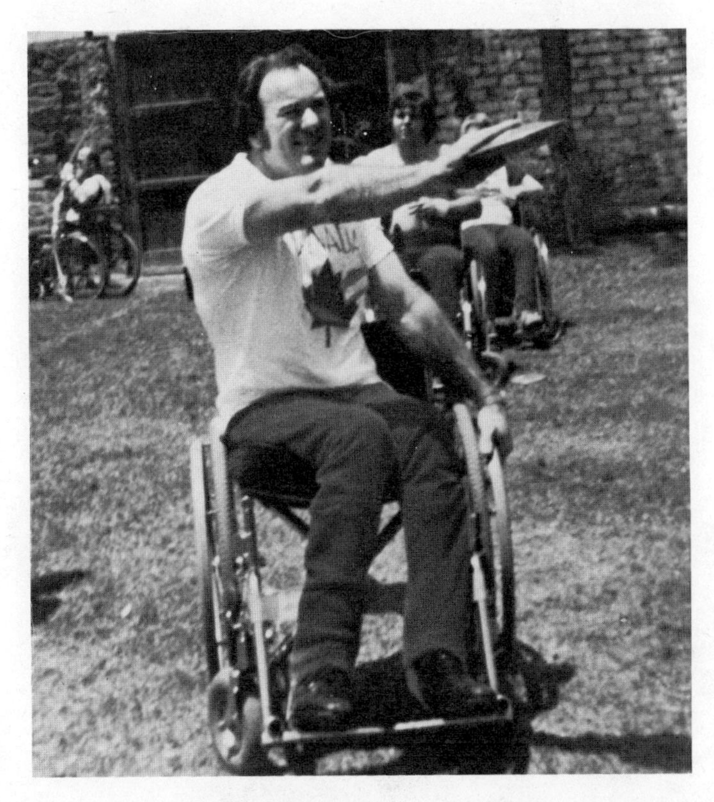

René Massé, paraplegic since 1969, is Job Placement Counselor for the Canadian Paraplegic Association, Quebec Division (Canada). René has won 39 medals nationally in six years. At the Pan American Games in Peru in 1973 he won a gold medal in the 100-meter race and set a record in the 400-meter race.

Club Throw

Sharon Long with . . .

and without her young son.

Javelin

Exquisite extension of one man's body as Ray Clark of the U.S. propels the javelin as far as humanly possible. (Eddie Coyle, middleweight weightlifter, observes from behind the fence.)

National Games for the Physically Handicapped In Bogotá, Colombia, November, 1974.

This 29-year-old athlete was paralyzed by a bullet wound while serving as an officer in the Sudanese army.

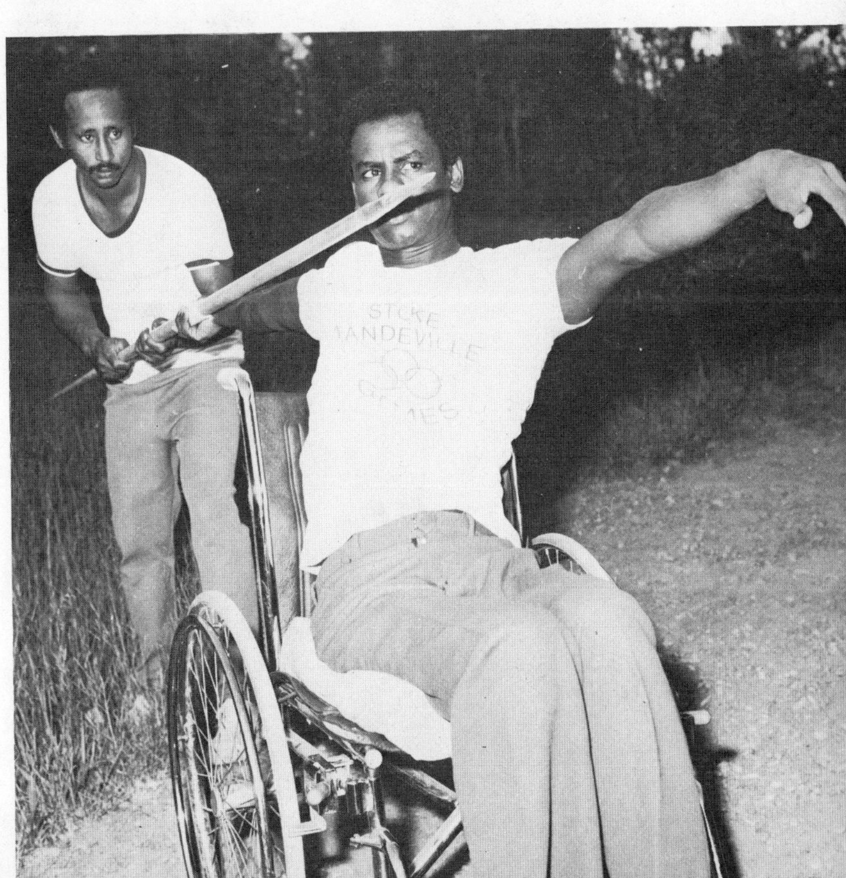

Different styles are used to hurl the javelin—some from the side, others overhead. (*Above,* Clarence Bastarache; *top right,* Tommy Hite; *bottom right,* Ed Batt.)

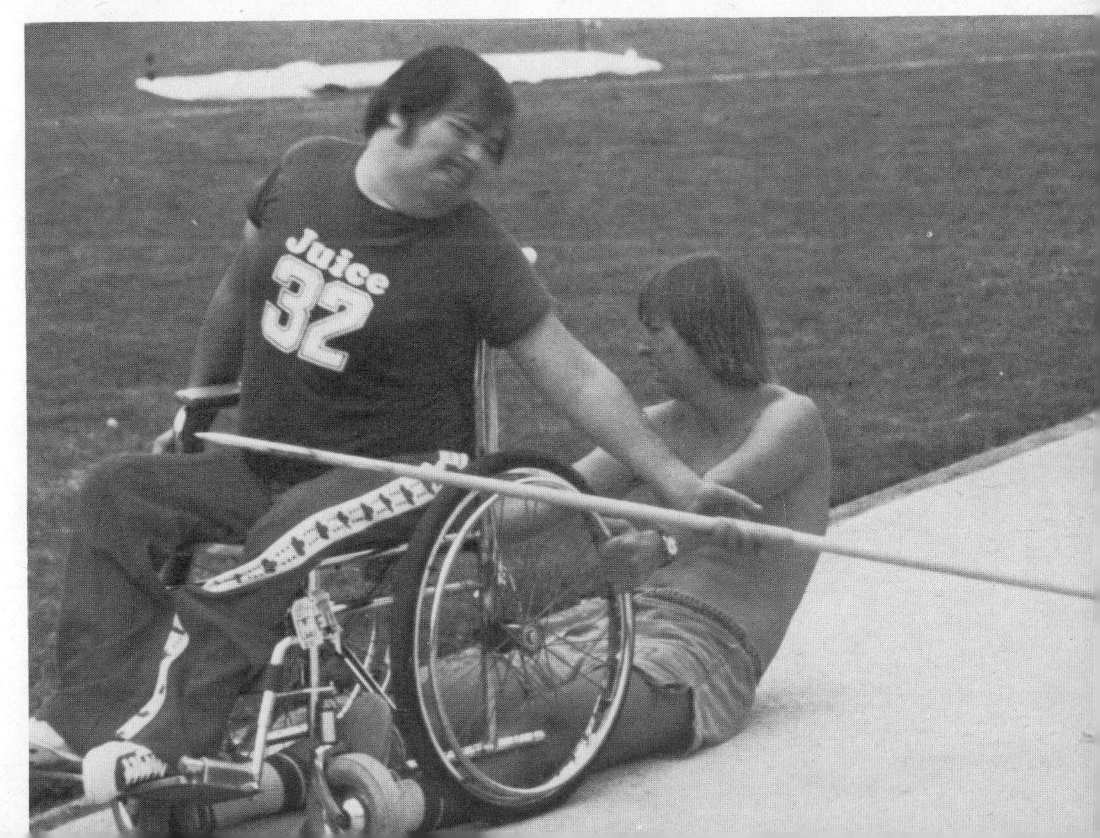
Juice
32

Time Out

Doug Lyons and Marilee Weisman. Says Doug, "I had my downs but sport helped me to get up."

Ben Reimer, from Winnipeg, was the only Canadian athlete to compete in the British Commonwealth Games held in Kingston, Jamaica, in 1966. He won a bronze medal in javelin.

Julius Duval with teammate David Kiley.

Members of the Swedish team with their three-wheeled chairs. They say they are more maneuverable; others say they are less stable.

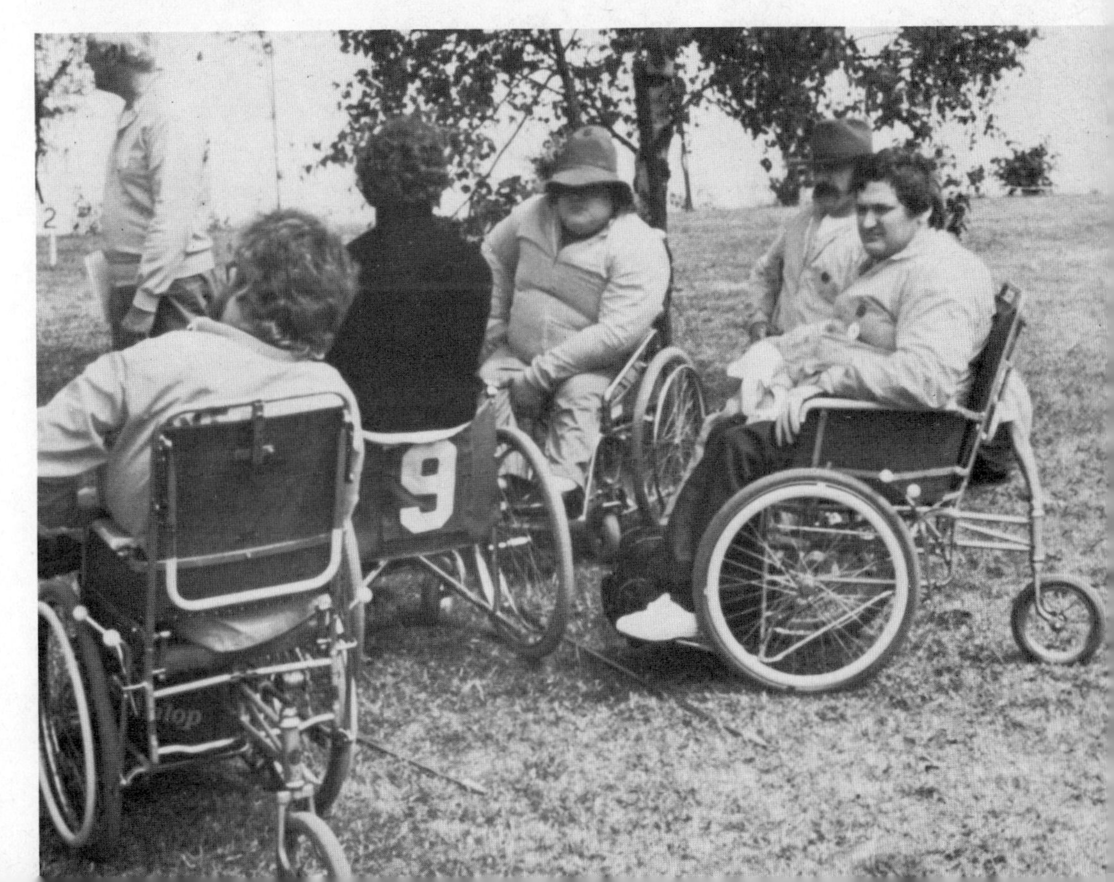

Lunchtime at Stoke Mandeville, 1975.

Frank Henderson at Stoke Mandeville in 1971.

Fatigue.

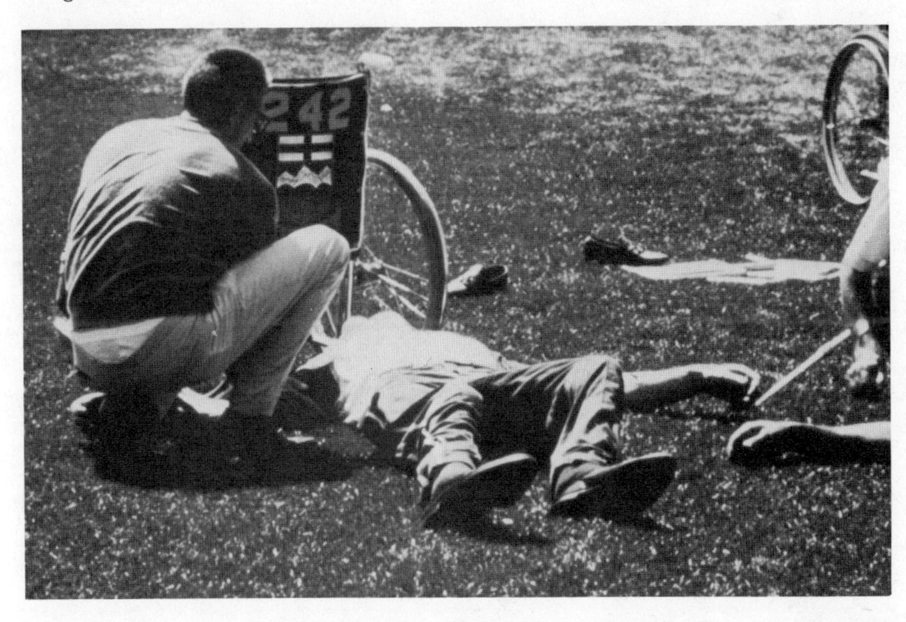

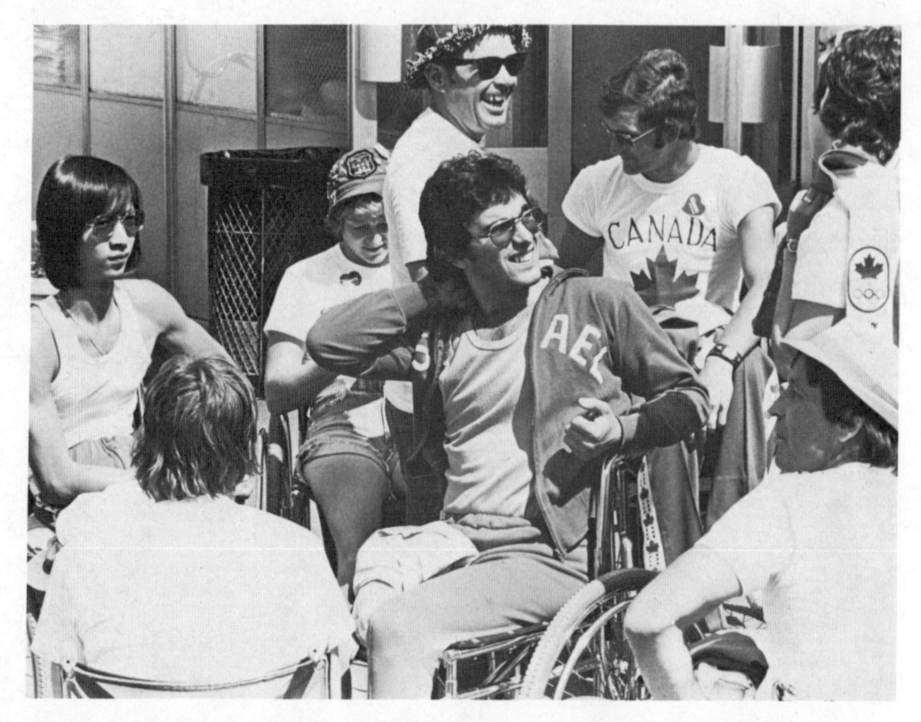

A crowd of Canucks. In the center Pete Colistro, track star, wears an Israeli jacket. The practice of exchanging apparel with members of other teams is very popular, particularly during the final days of competition. (From left: Leslie Lam, Diane and Tom Sharkey and Gunther Schuster. Standing behind Pete is "Boots" Cooper, the Canadian trainer.)

"The Pub."

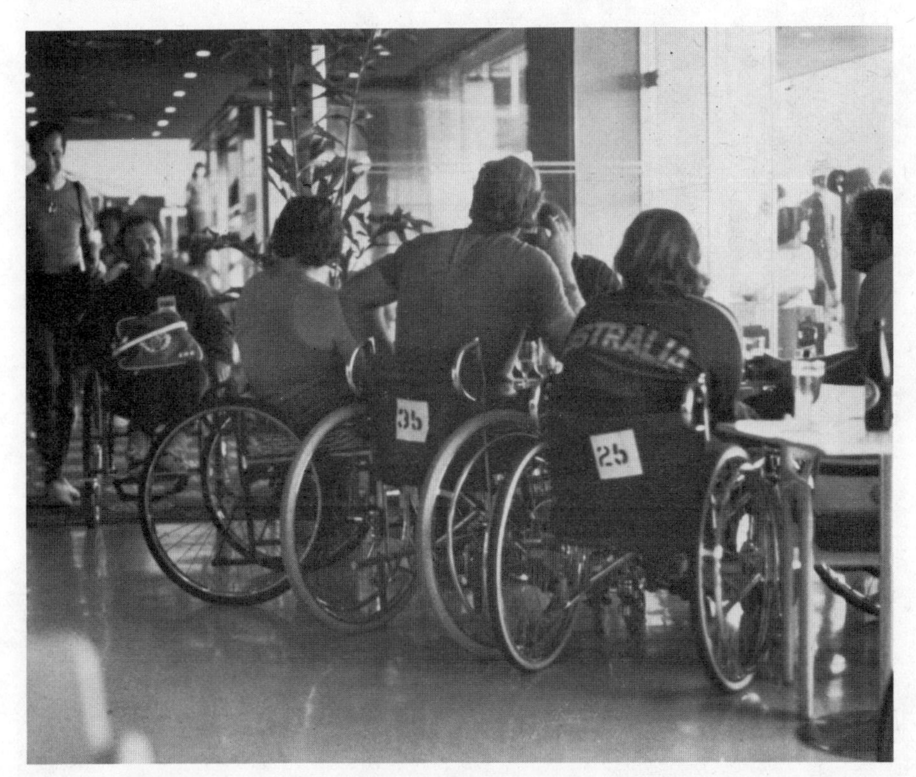

Table Tennis

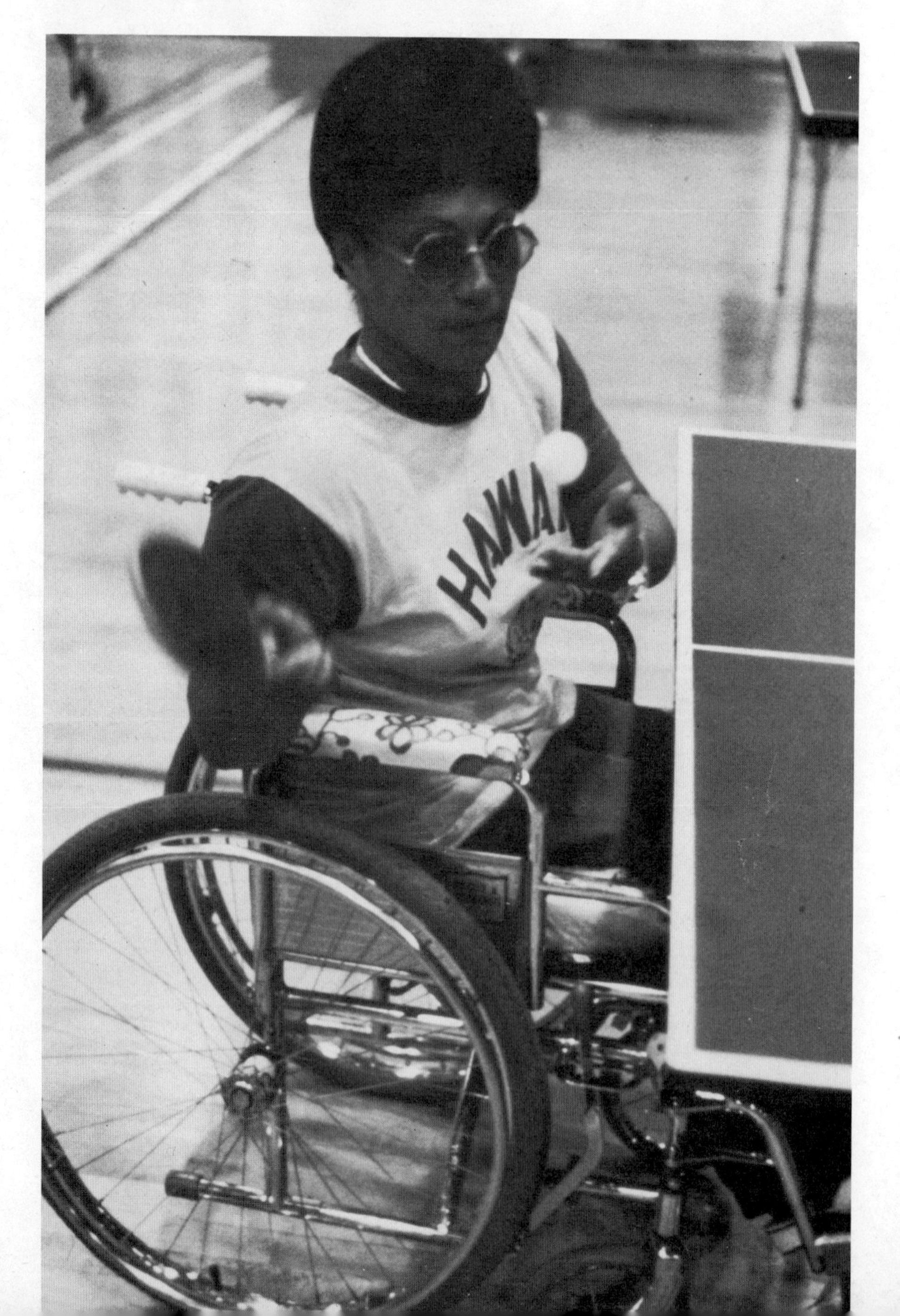

Table tennis players can compete successfully against standing opponents. Their main disadvantage is reduced mobility. Most competitors fix their wheelchairs in one spot by setting the brake. Between points they will sometimes move the chair to adjust to a change in strategy or simply to keep the opposition off balance.

Baruch Hagai of Israel is virtually unbeatable in table tennis because he keeps constantly in motion, using his free hand to maneuver the chair.

A standard type of chair is required. If it is built up to give the occupant a height advantage it is disallowed. Severe quadriplegics are, however, allowed to use a bandage to affix the bat to their hand.

Warming up for the competition.

Leslie Lam, born in Hong Kong, now a University of Toronto pharmacy student, competed internationally for the first time at 15 years of age. Leslie is shown playing against an able-bodied opponent. "If I play with someone standing up, it's better for my game."

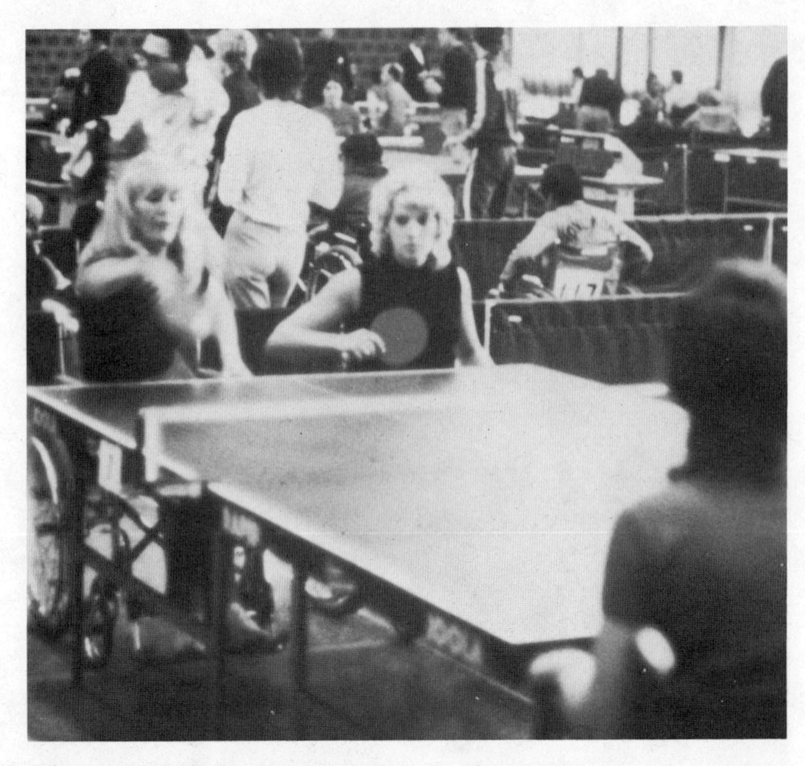

Irene Miller and Donna Wruth of Canada compete against Great Britain at the Paraplegic Olympics held in Heidelberg, Germany, in 1972. Irene *(left)* was in a car accident in 1953. In 1968 she was chosen "Manitoba's Sportswoman of the Year." Donna *(right)* currently holds Canadian records in her class for the shotput, javelin, discus, club throw, pentathlon and 60-meter race. She, too, was involved in a car accident in 1968.

Abebe Bikila of Ethiopia (former Olympic marathon gold medalist) became a quadriplegic as a result of a car mishap on a mountain road in Ethiopia. Because Bikila was a national hero and well-liked by Emperor Selassie, his involvement in wheelchair sports fostered interest among other wheelchair-bound people in his country. Bikila led a team of Ethiopian athletes to the 1969 I.S.M.G., where he competed in archery and table tennis. Mr. Bikila died in 1974.

Snooker

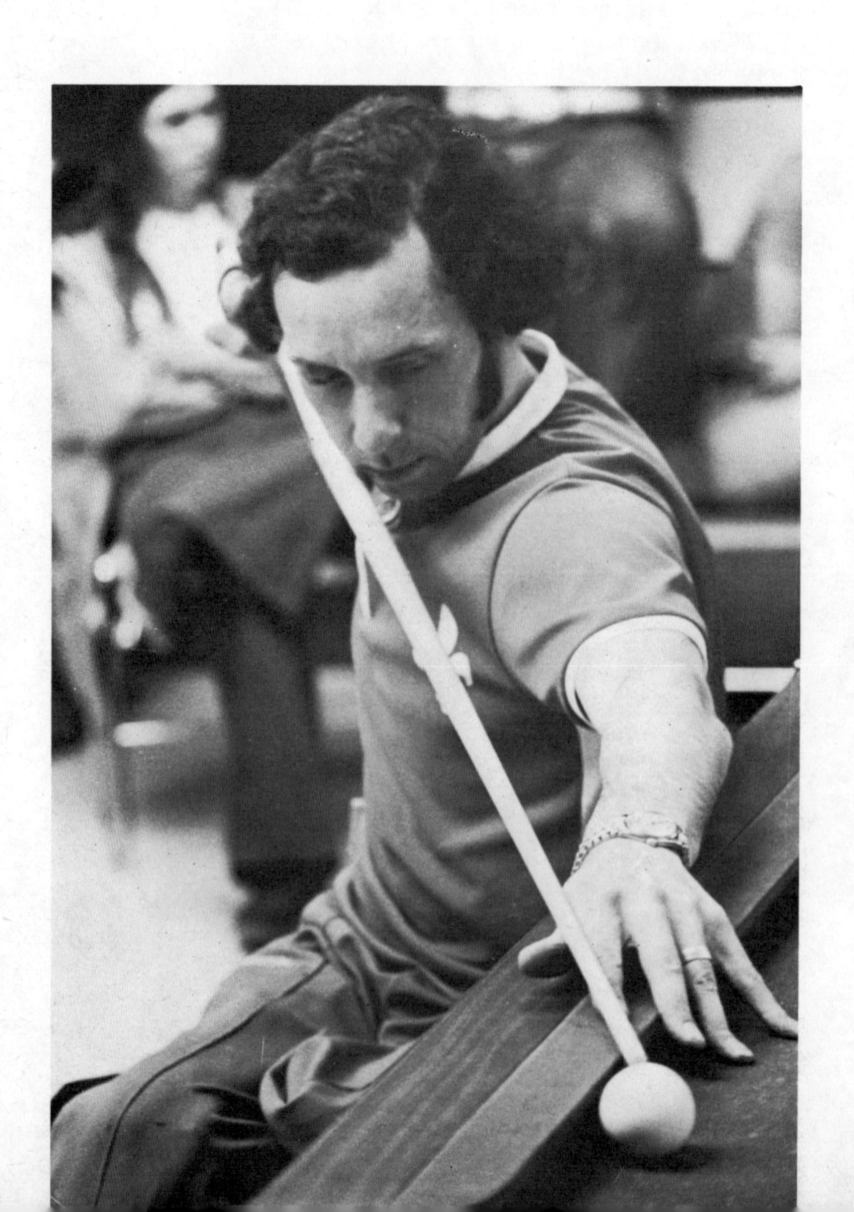

Most rehabilitation centers have a pool ta[illegible]
popular pastime. It is an activity that, lik[illegible]
joyed alone and practiced by severely dis[illegible]

At the games snooker competition seldom attracts large crowds. It usually takes place in a room set apart from the other events. The spectators are quiet and intense, many of them competitors themselves.

A rake takes on added importance for the disabled athlete, increasing his range and reach.

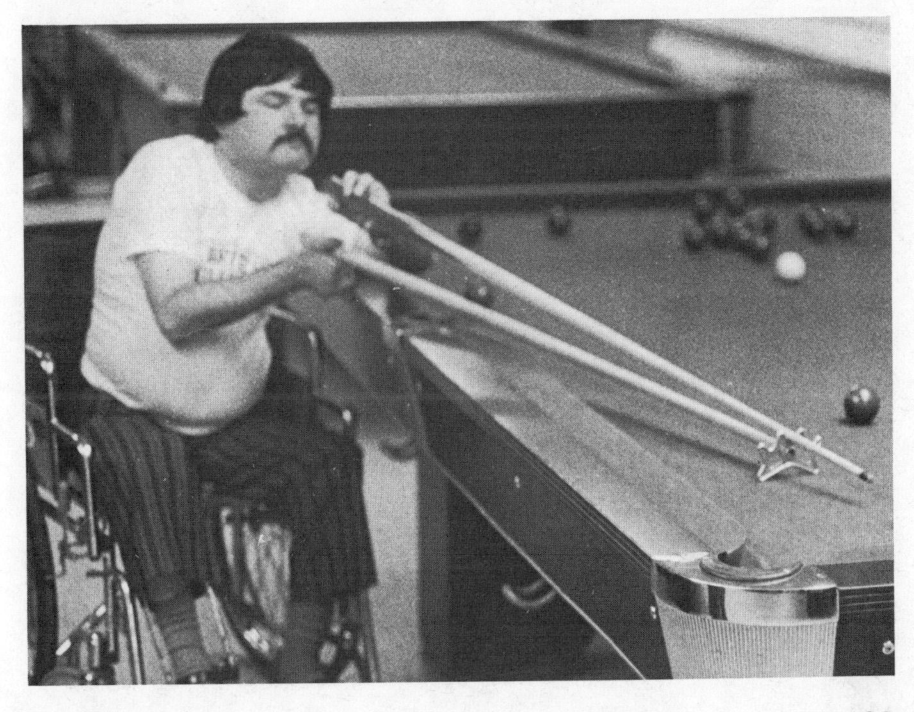

CANADA

Many consider slalom the wheelchair counterpart of the hurdles. The course is comprised of forward and reverse gates, ramps and obstacles. The technique that must be mastered by the slalom competitor is known as "wheelies." The athlete makes a backward or reverse turn of the wheels of the chair followed by a quick push forward. This results in a tipping back of the chair so that it is balancing on the rear wheels only. The technique is also useful in surmounting obstacles encountered in everyday life, such as sidewalk curbs and stairs.

Wheelies demonstrated by Connie Head of Rochester, New York, during a practice session.

Japanese athletes being run through the slalom course prior to competition. The man in the middle practices wheelies.

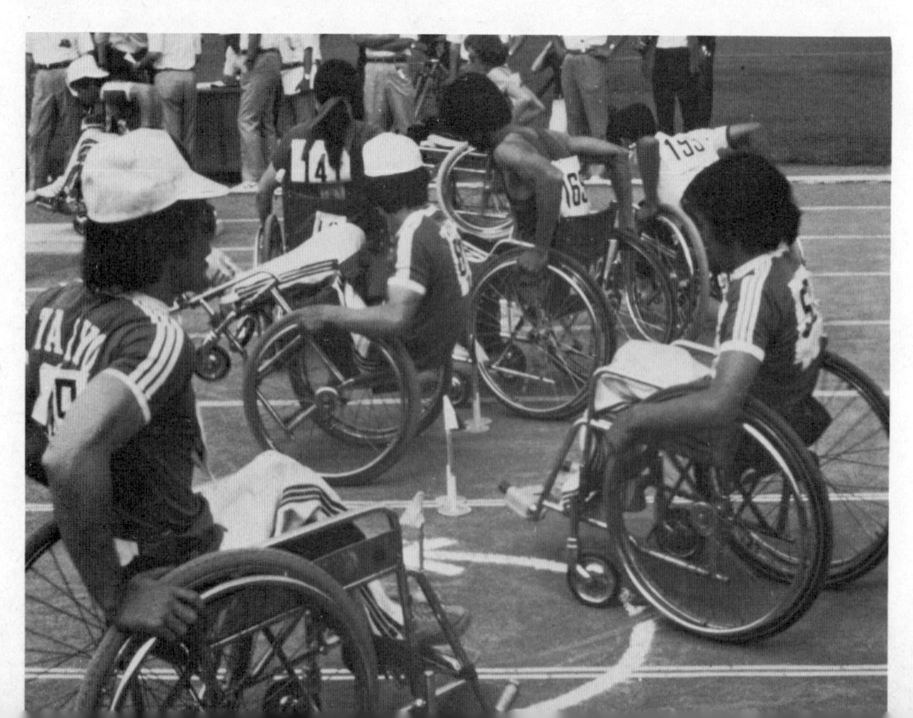

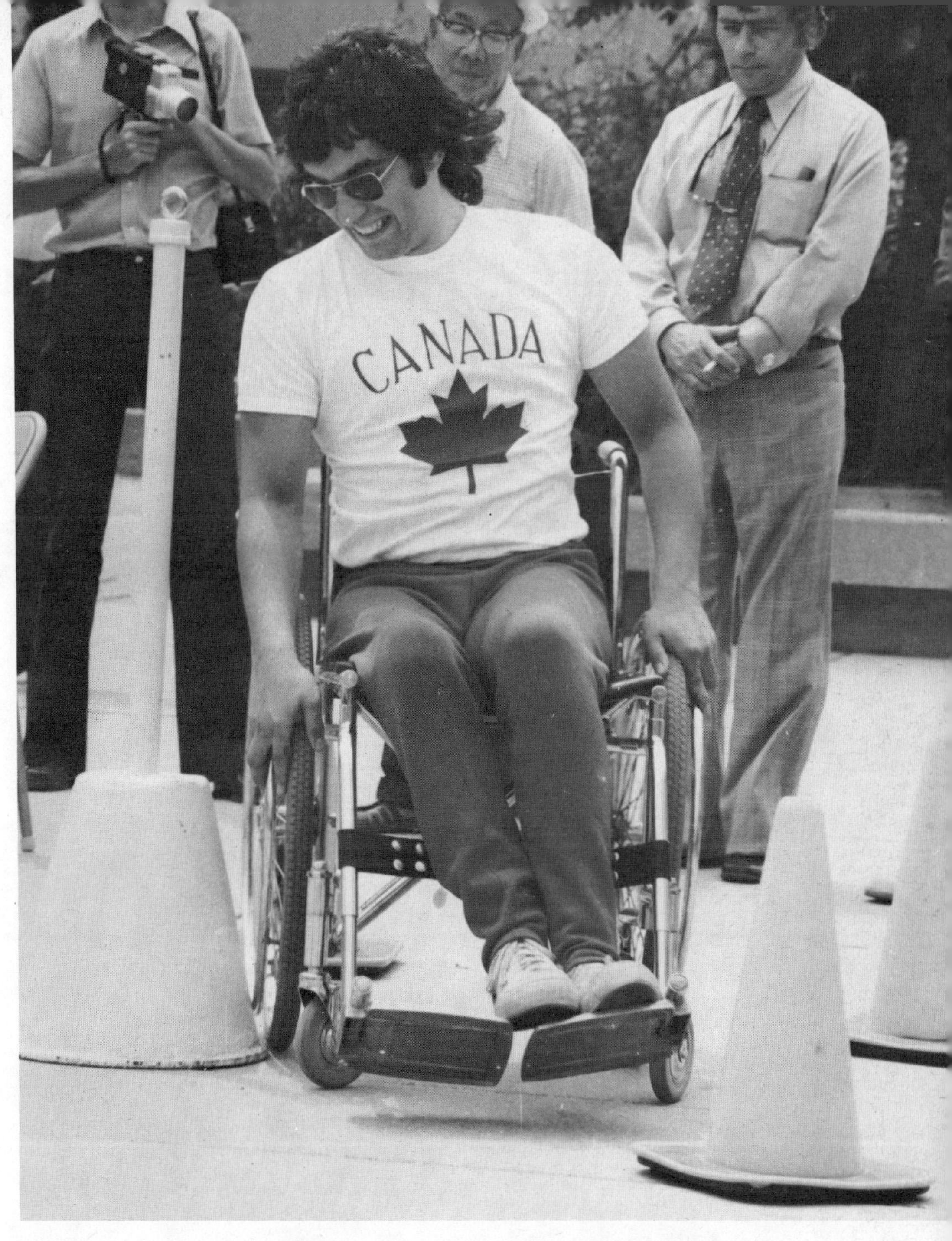

Peter Colistro gives a slalom demonstration at Toronto's City Hall in the summer of 1974. He has unofficially broken the six-minute mile and hopes to do so officially at the 1976 Olympiad. Pete's coach is a physical education teacher who applied the techniques of kinesiology (the science of human motion) to keep the wheelchair from veering off the track on corners, without losing speed.

Dennis Pottie tackling a ramp.

Weightlifting

Few competitions are as exciting as weightlifting. When a man who has never run in his life lifts 561 pounds and promises much more in the future, you can expect the crowds to assemble. The final heavyweight weightlifting event takes place last on the closing day of international games.

In able-bodied bench press competition, the athlete's arms are extended upward and the weight is placed in his hands. He lowers and then raises the weight.

In the disabled sport the athlete lifts the weight from the lower position upward and then down. This is believed to be more difficult than the able-bodied method, which benefits from momentum.

The athlete's legs may be held if spasm is present. If he refuses this assistance and one leg slips to the floor, the lift is not counted.

The participants in this event are handicapped according to their body weight. The winner in a particular division may lift a lighter weight but benefit by being a lighter man.

Kevin Earl, a paraplegic from Vancouver, who participates in basketball and swimming as well as weightlifting, is one of Canada's outstanding athletes.

Eddie Coyle, a 26-year-old athlete from Lansdowne, Pennsylvania, wears a brace on his paralyzed right leg to prevent it from buckling. He prefers to stay out of a wheelchair. Eddie, who contracted polio at age two is a middleweight champion weightlifter. He holds a Bachelor of Science degree in health education and hopes to become a physical and occupational therapist. He was, however, recently refused entrance into that university course on the grounds that he would not be strong enough to handle the patients.

A moment of decision in the featherweight weightlifting competition: Doug Lyons *(seated)* confers with a Canadian coach *(standing left)* and Dick Loiselle *(standing right)* prior to his third and final lift. Dick has worked diligently for disabled athletes. "Preferably, paraplegics would like to have their condition ignored completely, both in social life and employment. Their other qualities should be permitted to overshadow the wheelchair."

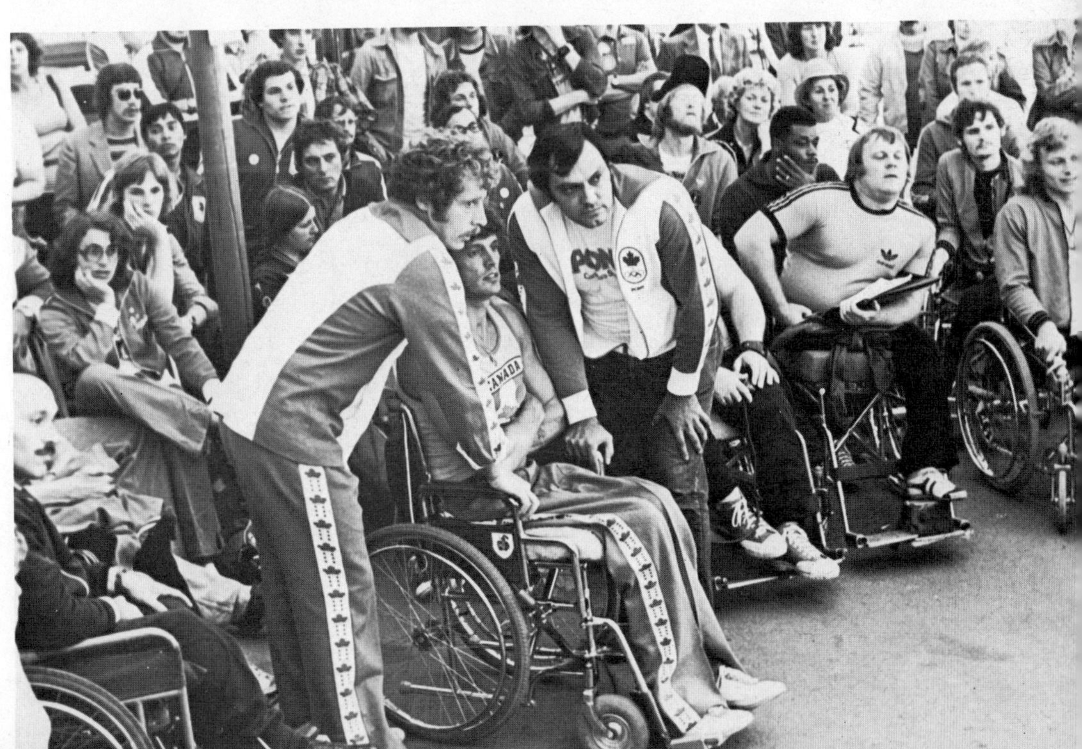

Jon Brown is a watch repairman from Rialto, California. "When I see someone more disabled than myself I'm turned on by the amount of work they do that I take for granted. I contracted polio in 1946. My physio brought me from a person who was completely paralyzed to my present state. He used to tell me that one day I'd be the strongest person in the world."

Question: "How would you describe the day of competition."

Answer: "You want to get your head together so you can control your body and go out and do the best you can. It takes a lot of concentration. And you can't have any distractions. You have to think of what the event means to you and the people that helped you." *Eddie Coyle*

"I don't remember walking. I've never climbed a stair. I've never run. So for me these games are a dream come true."

At the I.S.M.G. in July, 1975, Jon Lifted 528 pounds, setting a new world's record. One month later, at the Pan American Games in Mexico City, he beat his old mark with a lift of 561 pounds. "I was really pleased," Jon states, "but I plan to do more than 600 pounds on my third attempt at the 1976 Olympiad."

Jon relaxes with his son Jon Paul and his niece. "When people see you in a chair first they are shocked. Then they feel relief. They think 'thank God it's not me.' Then they experience guilt for having thought such a thing. And then they pity you. Like most of the athletes I hate that one.

"When you're disabled I think you develop your sense of feel, touch and tenderness more."

SUOMI

Fencing

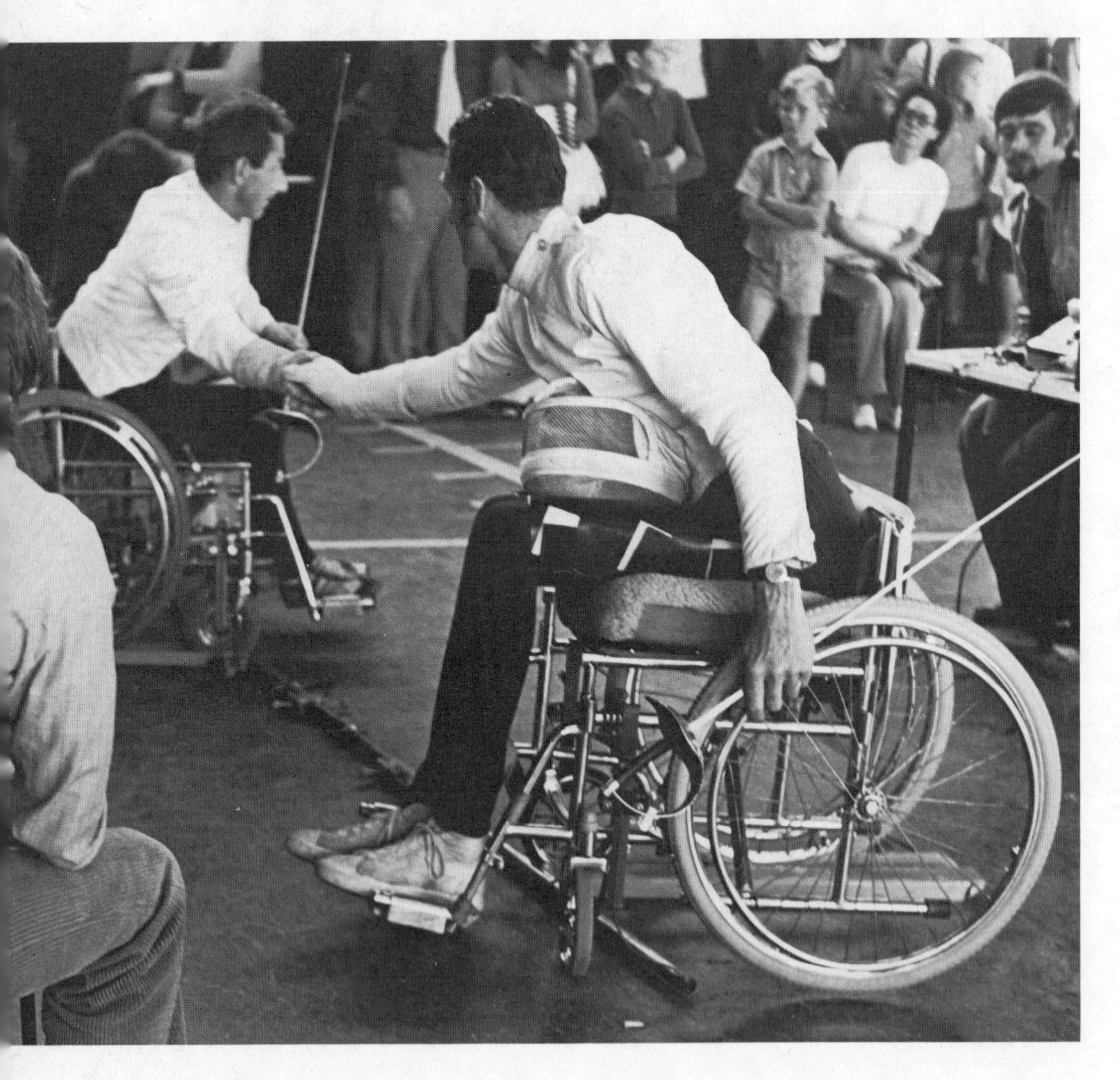

For many years Sir Ludwig Guttmann himself excelled in fencing. This may, in part, explain its inclusion in the Olympics. Canada will field its first team for the 1976 Olympiad.

Although fencing involves very little movement (wheelchairs are secured with a holding device), it is still one of the more unusual sports to watch. The referee speaks entirely in French and points are made so quickly that the untrained observer may miss them.

There is limited forward and backward movement of the body because the wheelchair is fixed in place with a holding device. Fencing helps develop balance, coordination, self-control and speed.

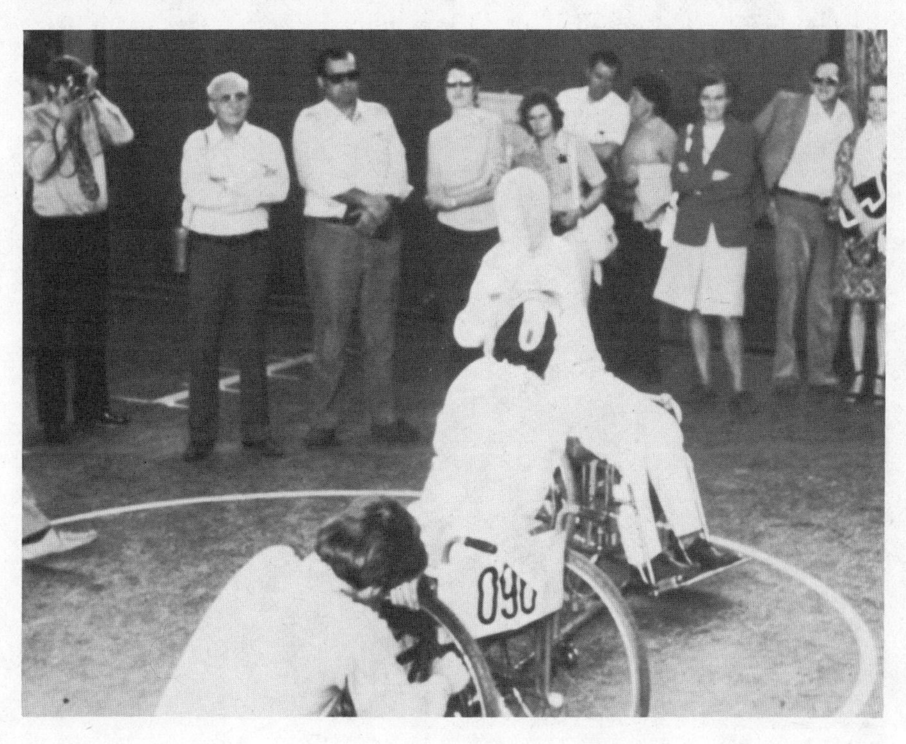

Bowling

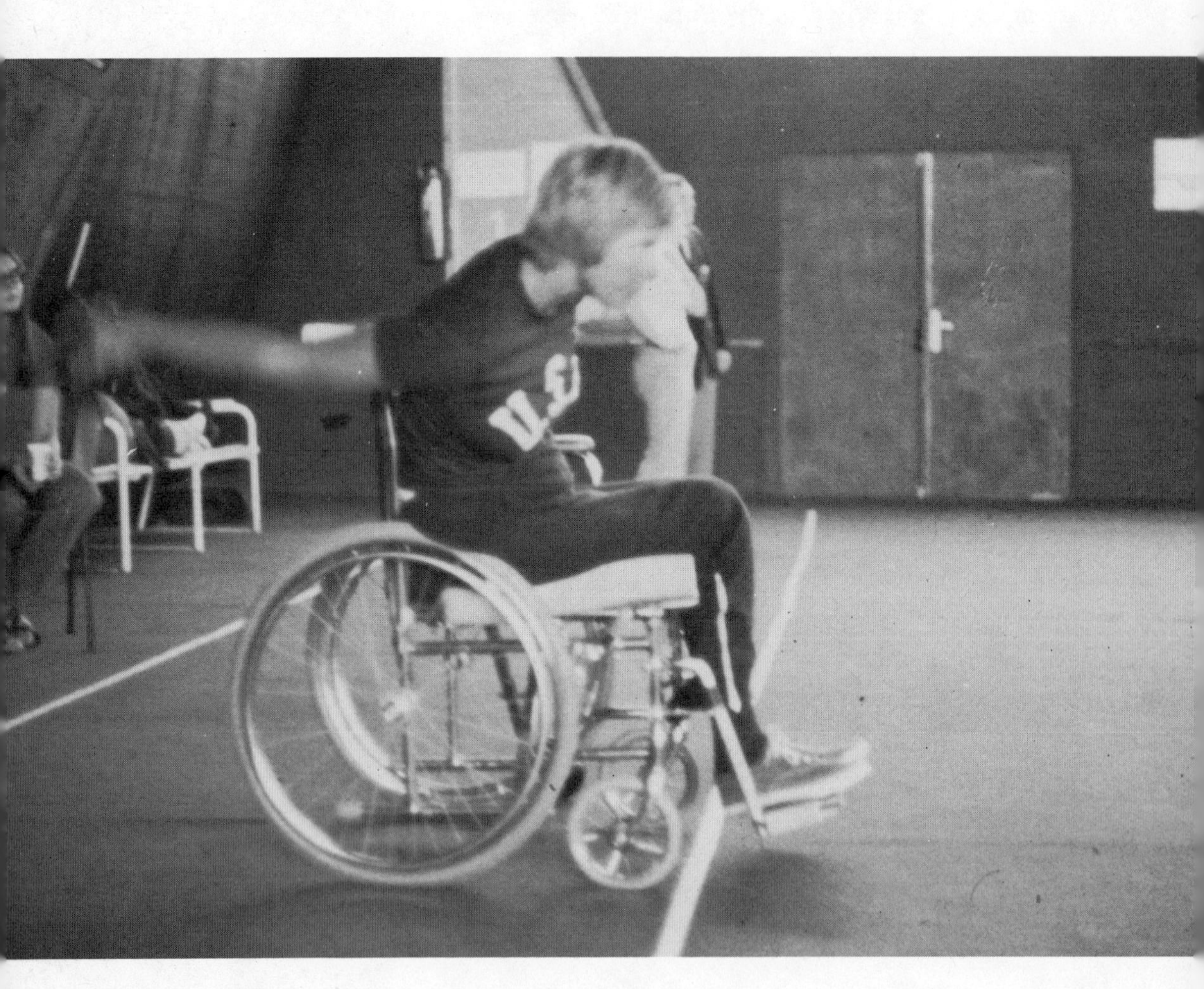

Bowling, also known as bowls or lawn bowling, [illegible]
doors or out. Since the player must lean forwa[illegible]
this sport provides good exercise for the lowe[illegible]
Rules are the same as for able-bodied lawn bo[illegible]
very gentle sport, bowling can be enjoyed by wheelchair athletes of
all ages.

105

Sometimes an individual who at first appears more severely disabled than others has an advantage in track events. Although he may sit very low in his chair with his head not much above the back of it, he can grab his wheels and turn them almost full circle rather than depending on the quick, short push method.

Track events include 60-, 100-, 400-, 800-, 1500-meter races and relays. The tag in all relays is made by touching the next person's arm between the shoulder and the wrist. Any verbal contact and the team is disqualified.

The world's record time for a Class-5-athlete 100-meter dash is 20.0 seconds. This was set by Ray Clark of the U.S.A. at the 1975 I.S.M.G.

The race begins as able-bodied races do. Only one false start is allowed per competitor. The racer must stay in his allotted lane, the front wheels of the wheelchair behind the line at the start and crossing the line at the finish.

Competitors at the starting line in Bogota, Colombia, November, 1974.

Jan Godfrey *(second from left)*, set for the start in Canada's national games (Edmonton, Alberta, 1968). "Having the opportunity to travel gave me more independence and reassurance. It got me out and away from the people I depended on."

Ray Clark reaches to tag teammate David Kiley during a relay race.

Ray Clark wins the 100-meter dash for a new Pan American record: 20.3 seconds. (Mexico City, August, 1975.)

"Wheelchair sports is an out. If you're uptight, you can wheel it out on the track. It's good for the body and the mind." *Hilda Binns*

Bob Simpson wins a gold medal in the mile race. (National Games, Montreal, Quebec, 1971.)

Nolla McPherson of Jamaica wins the 60-meter event (Class 3) at the Pan American Games in Lima, Peru, 1973.

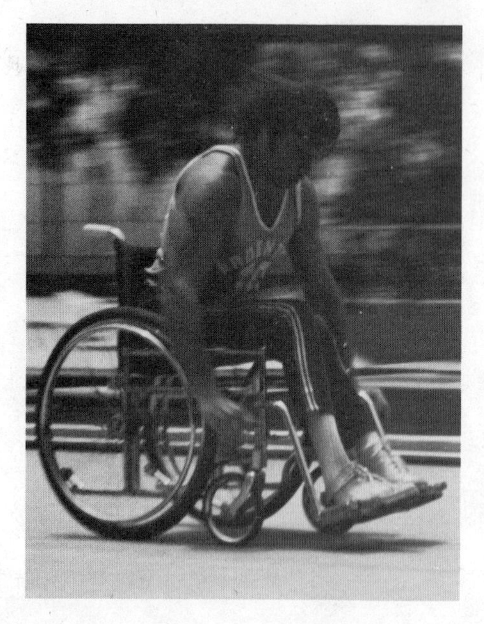

A smooth track is essential. Any stones or objects on the surface would cause the wheels to dig in and the racer to take a tumble.

"You have to keep moving; gotta keep the rust off." Tony Bagnato.

Neck and neck, a Brazilian and a Jamaican fight for the gold.

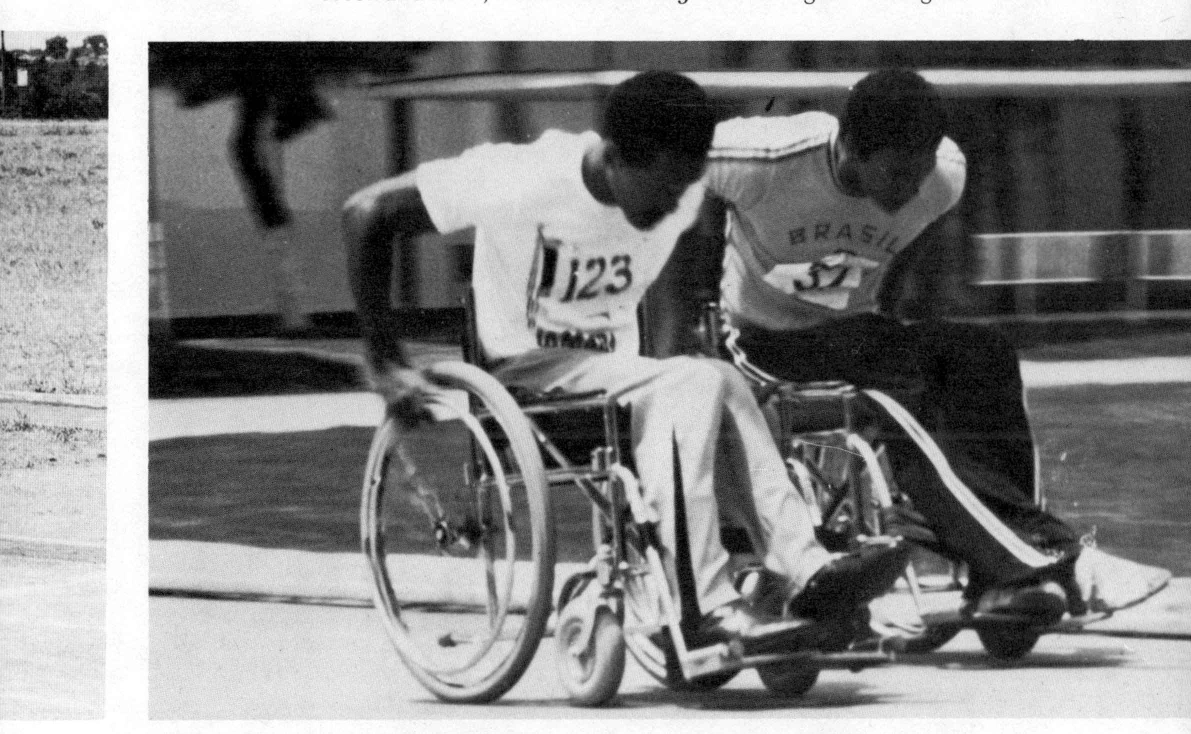

Richard Wasnock, born on September 28, 1941, contracted polio at the age of 12. Rich participated in local, national, regional and international games from 1967 on. At the Pan American Games in Peru, Rich won the award as the "Best Male Athlete of the Games" for 1973. On November 11, 1975, while on the way to play basketball in the U.S. North Western League, Rich was killed in a car crash.

"Arm work makes up for short legs," says Basil Grogono (Medical Director of the Canadian Wheelchair Sports Association). This man's short limbs in no way hamper his racing ability.

Wearing a band around his head to absorb the beads of perspiration, Eric Russell of Australia exemplifies the speed and physical endurance needed to participate in competitive racing. "For me wheelchair sports are a bonus for being in a chair."

"I was injured in a snow accident two years ago. Went roaring down a hill in an inner tube, got bumped into, spun around and hit a tree going pretty fast.

"The therapist at the hospital I was in came into my room and said, 'We want you for our basketball team.' At the time I said, 'Sure,' but I really thought I'd just be sitting in the house, staring out the window. If we could just get more people who *are* sitting in their houses to participate they'd be a lot happier. It'd really improve their self-worth." *David Kiley*

David Kiley winning a gold medal at the Pan American Games in Mexico City, 1975.

In 1972, awards were given to the top Canadian Amateur Athletes of the Year. The female winner was Karen Magnussen, an Olympic figure skater. The male recipient was Eugene Reimer, a paraplegic from British Columbia. At the Olympics held the same year Eugene set a world record in the javelin competition which still stands.

ARGENTINA AUSTRALIA AUSTRIA
BAHAMAS BANGLADESH BELGIUM BRAZIL
BURMA CANADA CHILE COLOMBIA
COSTA RICA CUBA CZECHOSLOVAKIA
DENMARK DOMINICAN REPUBLIC EAST
GERMANY ECUADOR EL SALVADOR EGYPT
ETHIOPIA FIJI FINLAND FRANCE GREAT
BRITAIN GREECE GUATEMALA HONG KONG
HUNGARY INDIA INDONESIA IRAN
IRELAND ISRAEL ITALY JAMAICA JAPAN
KENYA KOREA LUXEMBOURG MALAYSIA
MEXICO NEPAL NETHERLANDS NEW
ZEALAND NORWAY PAKISTAN PAPUA, NEW
GUINEA PARAGUAY PERU PHILIPPINES
POLAND PORTUGAL PUERTO RICO
RUMANIA SINGAPORE SOUTH AFRICA SPAIN
SWEDEN SWITZERLAND SUDAN TRINIDAD &
TOBAGO UGANDA UNITED STATES
VENEZUELA WEST GERMANY YUGOSLAVIA

PART THREE

Shalom

" No greater contribution can be made to society by the paralyzed than to help, through the medium of sport, to further friendship and understanding amongst nations." *Sir Ludwig Guttmann*

"Disabled athletes could teach the able-bodied some things: generosity of spirit, free exchange of assistance and camaraderie. Somehow the competitors in wheelchairs seem to have come closer to the Olympic ideal than their able-bodied counterparts."

Marilee Weisman

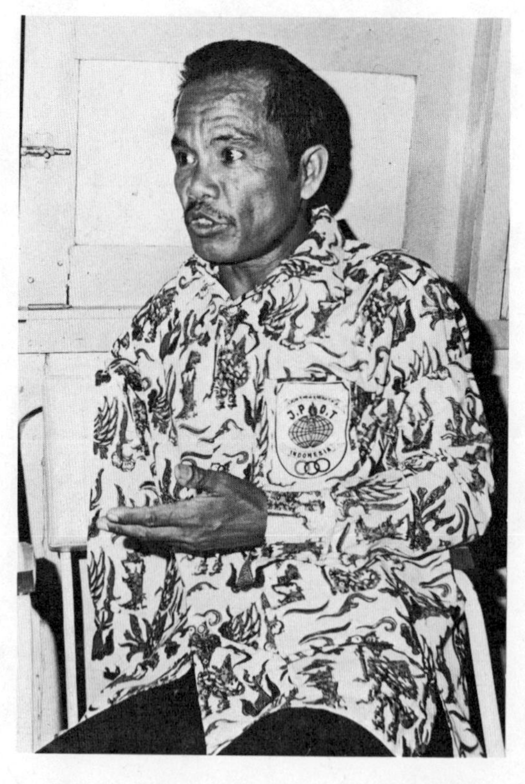

Mr. Pairan Manurung, founder of the Foundation for the Promotion of Sports for the Disabled in Indonesia, established in October 31, 1962. Mr. Manurung's involvement is more personal than one would expect. In 1952 a car accident resulted in the amputation of his right arm from above the elbow.

Andre Chiari of Switzerland.

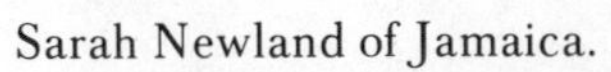

Sarah Newland of Jamaica.

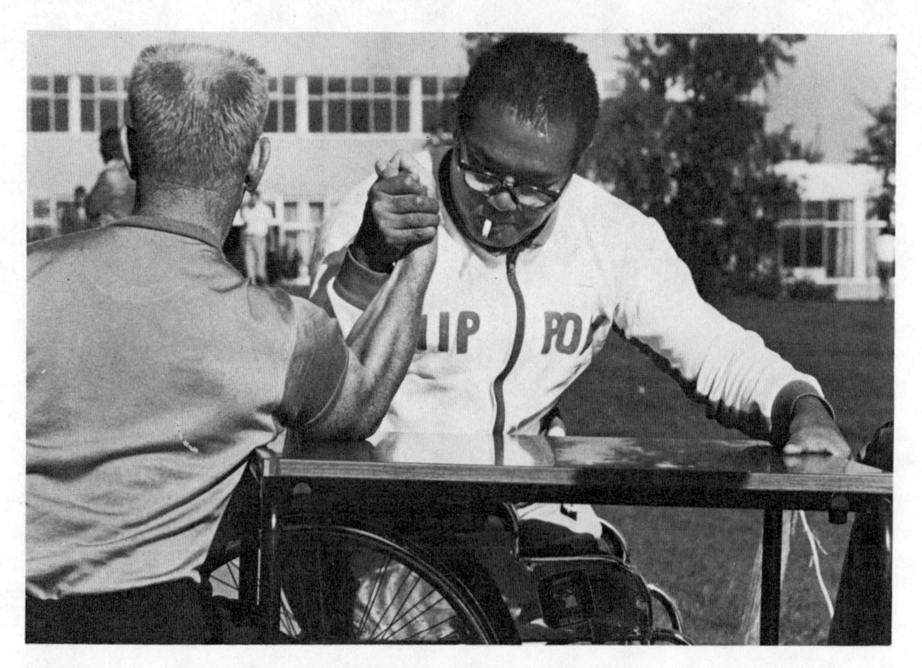

A Japanese competitor arm-wrestles with a Swedish coach in unofficial competition.

Ireland's bronze medal winner (Stevens) and Canada's gold medalist (Lyons) confer.

Dr. Robert Jackson, Chairman of the 1976 Olympiad for the Physically Disabled, relaxes at home. Dr. Jackson recently received a Civic Award of Merit from the City of Toronto for his efforts in furthering sports for the disabled.

Roger Mondor *(left)*, is Executive Director of the Fédération des Loisirs et Sports pour Handicapés du Québec and a Director of the 1976 Olympiad. He is shaking hands with Roger Rousseau, President and General Commissioner of the 1976 Montreal Olympics.

Sy Bloom, a physical education teacher who has been involved in American wheelchair sports for 20 years, looks over the shoulder of a Kenyan coach reading the local paper (I.S.M.G., 1975). During World War II Sy suffered leg injuries when hit by a mortar shell. "I was disabled myself but made a good recovery. I often said to myself that but for the grace of God I could have been confined to a chair for life."

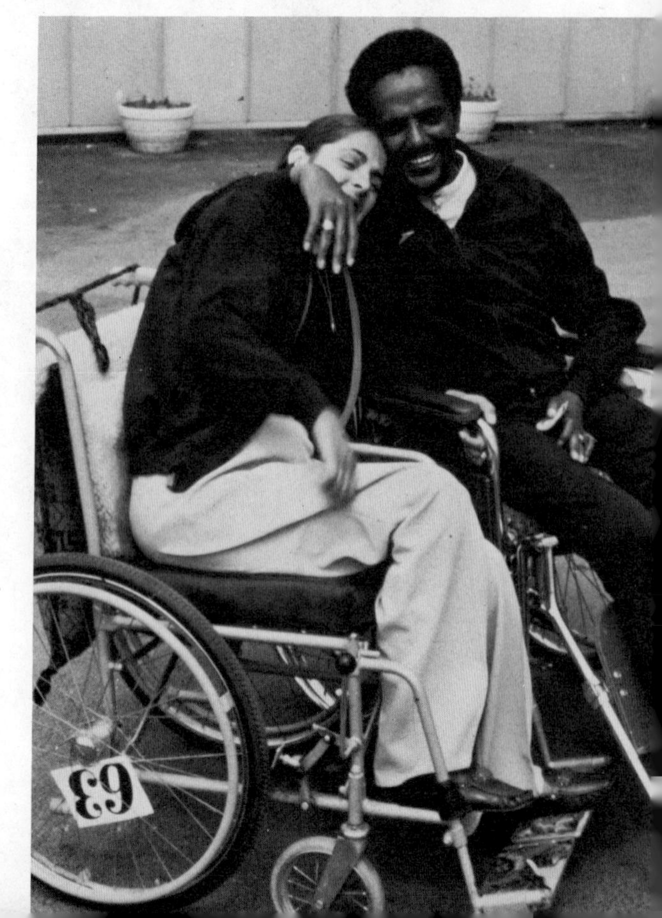

Britain and Ethiopia.

Sir Ludwig Guttmann, founder of sports for the disabled, was knighted in 1966 by Queen Elizabeth II for his efforts. He is seen here having his hat adjusted by Joan Scruton, his secretary and close associate since 1944. She says of Sir Ludwig: "He's the kind of man who expects 100 percent from those around him. But that's all right, because he gives more than that himself."

Wheelchair sports benefit all who participate. But they also aid those others confined to a wheelchair who are not athletically inclined, for they become a symbol for all paralyzed people. In addition, able-bodied viewers who note the extraordinary determination or talent or endurance of the athletes will change their attitude toward those in chairs.

Godfrey Sands of the Bahamas. Godfrey, now aged 16, contracted polio when he was two.

Though sports for the disabled have attained a very high level in terms of the quality of the competition, the variety of events and international involvement, they have reached merely a temporary resting place in history. Admittedly, there are special problems associated with conducting an international sports event for the physically disabled, but these have been solved by patient and judicious administrators. There is no longer any valid reason for holding the games at a separate time and in a separate place from the regular Olympics. Not until able-bodied and disabled athletes compete in integrated international competition will the Olympic ideal be fully realized.

Sir Ludwig Guttmann describes the four stages of the life of a pioneer, as he lived them:

"During the first stage people don't believe that you can do better than others.

"Stage two begins when individuals try to fight you and your views. At this point you have two alternatives: either you fight back or you pack up quickly. I'm a fighter from my early youth.

"Then comes the third stage. You are still unpopular but you are respected. You have shown that 'it can be done'; you have made the grade, you have introduced something revolutionary.

"And if you live long enough, as I have, then you are loved. And that is stage four."

Yearly competitions are held for the handicapped children in Indonesia. Here youngsters enthusiastically participate in a race that is an international favorite: a spoon full of marbles is balanced in each child's mouth.

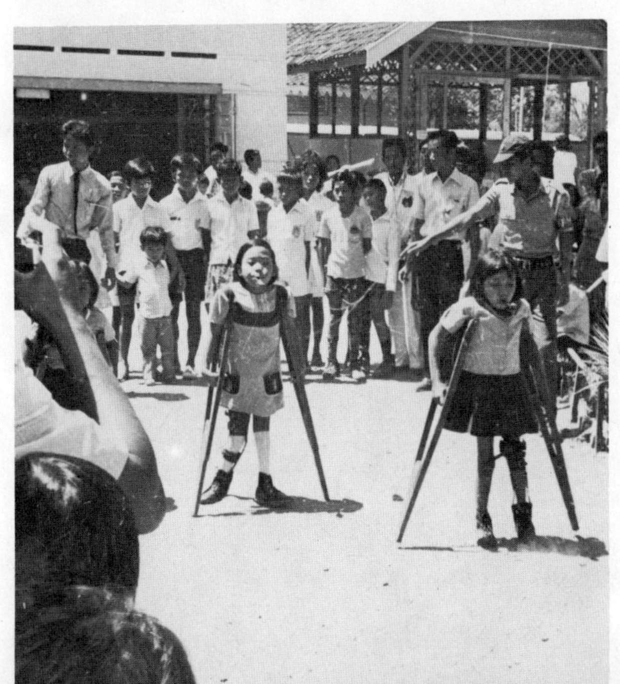

Acknowledgements

We wish to thank the Prime Minister of Canada Pierre Elliott Trudeau and the Department of External Affairs for all their assistance in obtaining international material during and after the 1975 postal strike with a minimum of red tape.

From the first time that our editor, Rick Archbold, laid eyes on the manuscript of *So Get On With It,* he has understood our aims and helped us to realize them. Thank you Rick.

Our gratitude goes out to all wheelchair athletes for you are the reason this book exists.

Jan Godfrey
Marilee Weisman

Photo Credits

Courtesy of the 1976 Olympiad for the Physically Disabled: pp. xvii, 32, 38, 39, 47, 48, 49, 50, 53, 62, 63, 66 (bottom), 67, 68, 72, 73 (top left), 80, 81 (bottom), 83, 85, 89, 92, 93, 95 (top), 96, 97, 98, 100 (top), 101, 102, 112 (bottom), 116, 119 (bottom), 120, 121, 128, 134 (top), 135, 136 (bottom), 137, 140, 142, 148 (bottom), 150 (Peter G. Robinson, photographer); p. 151 (Panda Associates Photographers, Toronto); p. 113 (Sport Ontario News, photographer); p. 44 (Pearce A-V, photographer).

Courtesy of Dr. R.W. Jackson: pp. 33, 81 (top), 94, 99, 104, 106, 107, 110, 114, 125, 126, 127, 130, 136.

Courtesy of Roger Mondor, Canadian Wheelchair Sports Association (C.W.S.A.): pp. 26, 45, 52, 55, 60, 70, 73 (bottom), 87, 133, 149 (bottom); pp. 118, 141 (left) (Roger Mondor, photographer); p. 61 (Wamboldt-Waterfield Photography Limited, Halifax, N.S., photographer).

Courtesy of Ben Lipton, United States National Wheelchair Athletic Association: pp. 82, 84, 115, 132, 134 (bottom left); pp. 65, 90, 131, 139 (Sven Doehner and Ian Bezsylko, photographers); p. 31 (bottom) (Ross Photos, New York, photographers).

Courtesy of Marilyn Jackson: pp. 76, 77, 112, 119 (top), 123, 149.

Courtesy of Sammy Henriques and Ralph Hill-Jones, Jamaican Paraplegic Association: pp. 56 (bottom), 75, 133 (bottom), 147 (bottom), 152.

Courtesy of Ross Beggs, Canadian Paraplegic Association: pp. 25, 28, 29 (bottom) (June Wianko, photographer); p. 29 (top) (M.J. Bent, photographer).

Courtesy of Pairan Manurung, Yayasan Pembina Olahraga Penderita Cacat, Indonesia: pp. 66 (top), 78, 146, 153.

Courtesy of Hannes Heuberger, Vereinigung der Querschnittgelähmten (Paraplegik Ergruppe ASPR), Switzerland: pp. 31 (top), 37, 147 (top).

Courtesy of Diane Crowe: pp. 40, 86, 100 (bottom).

Courtesy of Diane Crowe, Paralympic Sports Association, Edmonton, Alberta: pp. 34, 134 (bottom right).

Courtesy of Allan Menard, C.W.S.A.: p. 43 (Ian Christie, photographer); p. 64 (John Colville, Calgary *Herald*, photographer).

Courtesy of C.W.S.A., (Cruton Studios Ltd., Burnaby, B.C., photographer): pp. 54, 143.

Courtesy of Doug Wilson, British Columbia Wheelchair Sports and Recreation Association: pp. 73 (top right), 108.

Courtesy of Prof. Hector Ramirez, Servicio Nacional de Rehabilitacion, Argentina: pp. 57, 144.

Courtesy of Elias Petras: pp. 58, 105.

Courtesy of Dr. Basil Grogono, C.W.S.A.: pp. 95 (bottom), 109.

Courtesy of Valerie May Townsend, Fundacion Pro-Deportes en Sillas de Ruedas, Bogotá, Colombia: pp. 91 (top), 130 (top).

Courtesy of Sir Ludwig Guttmann, I.S.M.G.F., England: pp. 124, 141 (right).

Courtesy of Tom Szus-Curtis, Toronto: p. 22.

Courtesy of Ontario Wheelchair Games Council: p. 88.

Courtesy of Victor M. Santana Carlos, Centro de Medicina de Rehabiliatacão, Estoril, Portugal: p. 56 (top).

Courtesy of El Tayeb el Sammani, Morale Orientation Branch, Khartoum, Sudan: p. 91 (bottom).

Courtesy of Jon Brown, Joyce Flaker, photographer: p. 122.

Courtesy of Michelle Nolas: p. 148.

Courtesy of Marilee Weisman: p. 35.

Bibliography

KAMENETZ, HERMAN L. M.D. *The Wheelchair Book: Mobility for the Disabled.* Springfield, Illinois: Charles C. Thomas, 1969.

GUTTMANN, SIR LUDWIG. "The Stoke Mandeville Games," *Abbottempo,* Book 3 (1967), pp. 2-7.

LOISELLE, RICHARD T. "Wheelchair Sports: Development in Canada and Its Impact on the Rehabilitation of the Physically Disabled." Master's Thesis, Dalhousie University, Halifax, N.S., 1973.

BREGMAN, SUE. *Sexuality and the Spinal Cord Injured Woman.* No. 726. Sister Kenny Institute, 1975.

WILSON, MR. D.J. "Counselling the Person with Spinal Cord Injury on Sex and Sexuality." Paper delivered to Canadian Paraplegic Association Conference for Rehabilitation Counsellors, March, 1973.

LIBRARY
OF
MOUNT ST. MARY'S
COLLEGE
EMMITSBURG, MARYLAND
129347